Miracles & Extraordinary Blessings

Edited By Lynn C. Johnston

Whispering Angel Books

A Whispering Angel Book

Miracles & Extraordinary Blessings

ISBN-13: 978-0-9841421-9-4

Whispering Angel Books
7557 West Sand Lake Road #126
Orlando, FL 32819

http://www.whisperingangelbooks.com

Printed in the United States of America

Whispering Angel Books is dedicated to publishing uplifting and inspirational works for its readers while donating a portion of its book sales to charitable organizations promoting physical, emotional, and spiritual healing. If you'd like to learn more about our books or our fundraising programs for your charity, please visit our website: www.whisperingangelbooks.com

"Miracles happen every day, change your perception of what a miracle is and you'll see them all around you."

~ Jon Bon Jovi

TABLE OF CONTENTS

DEDICATION

This book is dedicated to the angels, seen and unseen, who guide our actions and teach us to appreciate the miracles and blessings that surround us every day.

ACKNOWLEDGMENTS

The creation and development of this book would not have been possible without the assistance of many people. I would like to thank everyone who submitted their heartfelt stories and poems for this anthology. With hundreds of wonderful pieces to choose from, each prospective contributor made the selection process far more challenging and rewarding than imaginable.

My deepest appreciation goes out to Julie G. Beers. Her opinions, support, and expertise were invaluable during this process.

INTRODUCTION

If you were to ask most people to define a miracle or extraordinary blessing, they would probably tell you about a financial windfall, an unlikely recovery from a life-threatening disease, or the birth of a child. While they would all certainly qualify, we often experience less dramatic blessings – and yes, even miracles – on a regular basis, if we choose to notice them.

While I was preparing this introduction, I reflected on our wonderful collection of touching stories, beautiful poems, and insightful quotes contained within these pages. Even though these pieces varied in subject and style, I couldn't help but notice that they all had one thing in common – a profound sense of gratitude.

In *Miracles & Extraordinary Blessings*, you'll experience the gratitude felt by our writers for the family and friends who lifted their spirits in difficult times, and for a loving God who heard their prayers and healed their wounds, physically and emotionally.

You'll feel their gratitude for the departed loved ones, guardian angels, and patron saints who reassured them that they and their loved ones were being watched and protected from above. And you'll read about the kindness of total strangers, like the nurses, motel owners, and newspaper delivery women, who became a blessing when they made the extra effort to aid our writers in their time of need.

These deeply moving stories and poems also celebrate the fact that our love and compassion for others can often be a source of blessings and miracles; simply giving an inexpensive gift or a kind smile can provide healing and restoration beyond our knowledge.

Finally, you'll share in the celebration of new lives, old friendships, and the realization that even nightmares can have happy endings.

I am reminded of a powerful quote by Suze Orman, "When you are grateful - when you can see what you have - you unlock blessings to flow in your life." To all of these talented writers, I would like to express my deepest gratitude for sharing your heartfelt stories and poems. Without your contribution, this book would not be possible.

I hope as you read *Miracles & Extraordinary Blessings*, you take time to reflect on the miracles and blessings in your own life – and you ask yourself what more you can do to be a miracle for others.

~ *Lynn C. Johnston*

"It's great to receive a miracle, but there's no better feeling than to become a miracle." ~ Joel Osteen

I BELIEVE
By Ranita Adams

I BELIEVE everything happens for a reason. Yes, even my diagnosis of cancer as well as the timing it all occurred. Last spring I got so caught up with work and planning our family vacation to Disney World that I neglected to take time out to schedule my annual mammogram. I did, however, fit in an appointment with my primary care physician for a complete physical. I wanted her to run every possible test there was on me. I had a feeling something was wrong. I am not sure why. My results came back and she told me I was the most boring patient she had. All of my blood levels were awesome! I was so relieved! Three months later I was diagnosed with cancer... HER2 positive invasive breast cancer.

I spent weeks beating myself up for not scheduling my mammogram on time. My doctor finally told me that with my type of cancer, they might not have found it 3 months earlier. Basically, my situation could have been worse. If the tests had not detected my cancer it might have had an entire year to spread even more. Also, had I been diagnosed, our trip to Disney would have been postponed for years. I am so happy my kids were able to have those memories just months before having to deal with their mom's battle with cancer.

Many of you may be facing your own battle. I do not have to explain to you the feeling of fear that overcomes you after being diagnosed. What opened my eyes the most was how everything else went on around me. The world does not stop because you have cancer. As a wife and mom, I could not imagine my husband and children moving on without me. That pain was unbearable. I was not ready to let cancer win.

It wasn't until I had a plan that I could actually pull myself together and start to fight. I was diagnosed on Friday and by Monday I was able to meet with my surgeon and oncologist. During our appointment my oncologist received the results of the type of cancer I was facing. This information was crucial to determine my treatment

1

options & severity. When she got off the phone with the pathologist, she smiled at me and my husband and said, "we got this." Not only did I leave her office with a plan, I left her office with hope and optimism. I BELIEVE without hope we have nothing. I was given hope that day and so my journey began.

Since that day I was determined to fight this disease with faith and courage. My Faith is the most important thing in my life followed by my family and friends. I would use that as my inspiration and motivation to beat this disease. I never asked God, "why", but I did ask, "what next?" I BELIEVE everything happens for a reason and I know he has a plan for me. Don't get me wrong... cancer sucks! But I BELIEVE God has a bigger purpose for me. I am not sure what that is yet. I heard the term, "We Got This" on multiple occasions, so I decided to make this the theme to my journey.

I had my port installed and started treatment the following week. I decided I would continue to work through my treatments instead of going on short term disability. I wanted to keep myself busy and surround myself with positive people. I needed prayers and encouragement and I could not get that from being home alone every day. I would mentally prepare myself for each chemo. My treatments became my game day. I had to get my "game face" on. I wore a different team jersey each time. My nurses looked forward to seeing what team I would show up in next. Whatever I could do to take my mind off the days to come and make it a positive experience. I felt so blessed just to be there. That meant I had hope. I BELIEVE your attitude is half the battle and I was determined to win that one. I have little kids. I wanted to be an example to them and show them you can stay positive no matter what challenges we may face. I still have a lot of love, laughter and life in me and cancer was not going to take that away.

In October, my family and some friends from San Antonio headed to Dallas to participate in the Race for the Cure. I had once lived in Dallas and many of my friends were still there. They wanted to walk for me and with me... and so Team Ranita was formed. It had been the most overwhelming and emotional part of my journey so far. People were there to remember who lost their battle, support those still fighting, and celebrate life for the survivors. It was the smiles from those survivors that gave me the strength I needed to cross the finish line two days after my 5th chemo. I will never forget that day and the hope those women gave me. I was inspired by their bravery. I was motivated by their strength and courage – as emotional as it was for me. I BELIEVE God wanted me to experience that for a reason. Some of these women were terminal. Cancer may have diminished their strength but it did not diminish their spirits and courage to fight. These women were amazing!

I felt blessed for the experience. Team Ranita finished the race in record time... 1 hour and 32 minutes. Ha ha! What a great memory!

Since being diagnosed, I have conquered 9 of 18 chemo treatments, eye surgery, a single mastectomy and completed 5 weeks of radiation. I am about to start the first reconstruction followed by my second mastectomy. God has shown me how truly blessed I am. My family is my "rock" and has been amazing. My husband has never once complained or sighed for having to take care of me and my kids through all of this. My kids have been my inspiration. It saddened me for them to have to see me go through this. Some days being worse than others. Through it all, they have encouraged me and made my heart smile in so many ways. We have also had the most incredible support group. People have reached out to us from everywhere. The friendships I have made and built along the way have been amazing.

If you are currently on a cancer journey as well, I am sorry you are having to go through this. I have learned that every person's journey is different, as well as the way they deal with it. You have to chose the right path for yourself. I pray you find strength and peace in your journey. It is not easy! The days are long and they are hard. But I BELIEVE attitude is half the battle. Be positive! Stay optimistic and surround yourself with positive people. They will encourage and support you. Remove or distance yourself from people in your life that may hold you back. Try to find the "can" in cancer.

I did not choose cancer... it chose me. But I refuse to let it consume me or define me. However, if I could use it as a platform to inspire others someday, I will gladly do so. I do BELIEVE everything happens for a reason and I will anxiously await God's plan for me.

We Got This!

Previously published on *alamocitycancercouncil.org*

HE HAS RISEN
By Sharon S. Fulham

Mary wept outside the tomb,
blinded by despair;
She did not see her Savior
Alive and standing there.

When He gently spoke her name,
she knew that it was true.
She gazed into His loving eyes
and faith was born anew....

Sometimes grief can be so great
that all one feels is pain –
Blinded by hopeless tears,
faith they can't regain.

The Savior longs for all to see
beyond distress and care.
See Him just as Mary did,
Alive and standing there.

Weeping may endure for a night,
but morning dispels the gloom.
May we behold a risen Lord,
not a darkened tomb.

SHIMMERING ANGELS
By Ronda Armstrong

One February afternoon, while recuperating from major abdominal surgery at home in Des Moines, I picked up the phone to hear a girlfriend's upbeat voice: "We're headed your way to drop off a surprise!"

I had no idea what. For years we supported each other as social work colleagues. Now retired, we nurtured our friendship with frequent phone calls and e-mails, celebrated special occasions, and met for coffee or brunch. When my rare tumor disorder flared up she sent uplifting cards, jotted funny emails, posted others on my progress, delivered food, and called every few days offering to run errands.

A few minutes later her husband, bundled against the chill, covered the walk to the front door in a few long strides. With a smile he handed in a gift sack. "Here you go!"

Inside a sheer fabric bag stood a battery-operated candle, an angel seven inches high. Silver glitter dotted the outlines of her wings and white flowing garment. After my husband Bill inserted batteries she lit up from within. That evening we turned on the timer. Our new angel emitted a soft glittery glow in the winter darkness until she shut off five hours later.

The angel stood on the back of the piano in the living room, and even though we knew of her presence, she surprised us every evening when she started to shine. Gazing at the flickering light, we absorbed her hopeful rays. Not only did she lift our spirits, she signaled us to pause and remember our friends who gave her to us, and countless others who blessed us with their caring expressions. The little angel cast miracles of light over us day after day.

Several months later, one of my cousins in Kansas began intensive rounds of treatment for breast cancer. I knew exactly what she needed.

I called my angel friend. "How can I buy an angel to send to my cousin?"

5

She gave me the ordering information. When I located the item online, the angel lights came in sets of three. I ordered two sets, not entirely sure how I would use them all. When the shipment arrived, I removed an angel, carefully wrapped it, and made a special trip to the post office, while praying and thinking positive thoughts about my cousin.

Not long after, late one autumn afternoon as supper aromas started filling the house, I grabbed the ringing phone.

"This is your cousin, who almost never calls! My angel arrived today. She's glowing right now!"

While stirring my concoction on the stove, I shared the story about how receiving an angel encouraged Bill and me to remember those who cared about us. "Now when she turns on every night we'll think of you and your angel too."

"Same here," she said. "Love you guys!"

When the holidays arrived soon after, Bill and I wrapped several angels for loved ones, a fitting gift for those who faced challenging times. When spring was on the horizon, we drove across the awakening landscape to visit friends who farmed. They had experienced a string of tough health issues, so now a shimmering angel stood watch in their living room too.

A few months later on Memorial Day weekend my cousin called once more.

"Where can I get an angel?"

She planned to give one to a friend when he entered the hospital for a bone marrow transplant. "He and his family really need an angel!"

Another day Bill planned to visit a longtime friend whose sons were visiting from out of state. Not knowing quite why, I had handed Bill an angel as he flew out the door. "Here, bet an angel would be welcome there." A few minutes after Bill arrived at the house, his friend's wife arrived concerned about her mother who had just been hospitalized. Months later these friends shared how the angel's comforting light was part of their night time routine. She'd incurred a wing injury, but even in her imperfect state she kept shining.

The special angel in our household continued to still shine brilliantly from her spot on the piano. The burst of joy she emitted when she glittered in the darkness had not waned. With more medical challenges surfacing for me after she took up residence, her meaningful presence as a beacon of hope and support grew even more.

One day while talking to my friend, I asked "Do you have any idea what you started? So many more angels shine bright since the one you gave us."

"Good to know angels keep shimmering," she mused.

She may not have predicted the full impact of giving an angel, but her kind act illustrates how miracles sometimes unfold in mysterious ways. Small gestures leave big impressions and influence a ripple effect of caring gestures like the angels casting miracles of light and love, connecting people through hope-filled presence.

The spread of angels with glittery garments, miles apart, shimmering in darkness, convinced me to never underestimate the ways compassionate acts move others, or the hopeful presence of angels who shine in our midst.

OLDER BLESSINGS
By Louise Webster

I just became a grandmother
It's hard to believe that's true.
I thought I'd seen most everything,
Yet this joy is new.

I've rocked my own two children
Felt my heart melt into theirs.
I would give my life for them,
Lay my soul full bare.

Mine was a deep fulfillment,
Love with no conditions.
Care that only multiplied,
And never knew division.

My son hands me his tiny daughter,
Hovering just a bit.
What I feel is overwhelming,
There are no words for it.

She is my child's child
She brings wonder, peace, and bliss.
My older age sees brand new purpose
How miraculous a gift.

ANGEL ON THE GROUND
By Lynn C. Johnston

When the world begins to crumble
And my wings can't take off in flight
Your gentle love envelopes me
Until I know I'll be alright

Somehow you lift me up
And help me learn to fly again
You guide me with a love
That knows no boundaries or an end

And when the world is on my side
Life goes as I think it should
You're the first to say, "Let's celebrate"
Or "I always knew you could"

You're my angel on the ground
My slice of Heaven from above
The special gift God sent me
So I'd always feel His love

You're such a cherished gift to me
I can't tell you what you're worth
Except to say you're living proof
Angels do live here on Earth

Previously published in *Angel's Dance: A Collection of Uplifting
& Inspirational Poetry* (Whispering Angel Books)

STILL WITH ME
By Daawy

It was quite ironic that my husband, sisters, and I were watching a comedy when the phone rang. My husband's cheerful face suddenly turned pale after he answered my dad's call. "What's wrong?" I asked.

"Nothing." My husband disguised a cool and composed look in front of me. He became awfully quiet then rushed to the bathroom for several minutes. I had a nagging feeling that something was terribly wrong.

I was nine months pregnant with my first child. Besides the agony of riding a rollercoaster of temperamental pregnancy hormones that took me by surprise, it did not help that I was the only one clueless. My family remained tongue-tied. They feared depression would induce my labor, but they merely fed the holes of anxiety in my heart with confusion and alienation.

After constant begging, my sister finally broke the news to me: Aunt Foziya passed away. I bathed several times during the day letting the water in the shower muffled my cries. No wonder my husband kept disappearing in the bathroom while we were happily watching comedy. With great struggle, he was freeing the sickening feelings — he skillfully wore in front of us.

Only a week earlier, my dear aunt sat next to me on the blue sofa in my home and said, "I hope you give birth today." I was frightened by her comment since I was not due yet. I later understood that she was destined to utter these words. She would never see my child after all. The last present she bought was a beautiful gold bracelet with black precious stones for my unborn son. It was believed to protect infants from envious eyes.

Aunt Foziya was a strong and beautiful lady. She suffered from asthma for most of her life. Even with her deteriorating condition, she was more than capable of managing all the affairs of her home and school — she was a school director. Unfortunately, the cortisone her doctors prescribed gradually doubled and tripled her weight, leading to a series of other illnesses. She tediously climbed the summit of Mount Everest every time she breathed and moved. It broke our hearts to watch her suffer.

My beloved aunt never married nor had any children. She considered me her daughter. When I was a child, she was the only grownup who allowed me to teach her a foreign language. She even patiently answered the tests I created for her. She once looked at me with eyes full of sympathy and said, "You're sensitive just like me. Balance your vulnerability to protect yourself." She managed her sensitivity quite well by laughing at herself and spreading soothing and contagious smiles to our hearts. When my sister remarked about herself that she was old, my aunt replied, "If you're old, then I belong in a museum."

The smoky, enticing aroma of green lentils, pasta, rice, caramelized onions and tomato topping, danced around my aunt's home whenever she anticipated my visit. My favorite Egyptian dish — Kushari — along with a Singaporean vegetable noodles — awaited me. My seat was always reserved next to her on the sofa. After I got married, my husband and I visited her more frequently. I bought her a huge box as a surprise and filled it with religious CDs, inspirational novels, designer perfumes, and dates. I wrote her a letter — my first attempt to share my writing with family. She cried happy tears. I told her we should meet weekly to discuss the novels and listen to the stories and songs in the CDs. Unfortunately I was bedbound, as my pregnancy took a toll on me. The regular visits never occurred.

In my religion, seeing the dead in dreams was considered real divine dreams — a blessing from God. This explained my excitement when I dreamt my sweet aunt as a little child falling down, shortly after her death. Mom said, "To God she was an innocent child and this was exactly how she died, tumbling like a child."

My dear aunt visited me again after I gave birth in hospital. I dreamt her grave was ajar and her eyes were wide opened. I screamed in horror, as it dawned on me that she was really gone. When I woke up, I was washed with light relief. God understood how miserable I felt. He brought her to me and showed her my baby. She saw my son after all.

I began to look forward for her "visits." The miraculous messages she brought me from heaven became more constant in times of trouble and dire need. God sent her to me in my sleep. Even after death, she was still alive within me and aware of all the difficulties that surpassed me.

I could never forget the time I spent the whole day getting rid of my things. These tangible objects held many painful memories. I decided to give them away to charity instead of trapping them in cupboards and drawers. It was a painful task since I had a bad habit of attaching myself to the past. Though not ideal, it made me feel secure. Some time had passed since I had seen her in my dreams. I prayed to God to make me stronger and pleaded with him to let me see my aunt once again in my dreams. I also whispered conversations to my aunt in the process. I told her how much I loved and missed her.

The next morning, my sister called me. She said, "I dreamt Aunt Foziya said that you were asking God to see her and then you sat with her in her living room and had a private conversation."

Tears formed puddles on my cheeks and drenched my dress. My prayer was granted. God's mercy engulfed me at every twist and turn in my life. Sunshine beamed at me in the form of my beloved aunt. She cleared the fog of ambiguity from the mirror of my days by illuminating my path. She was still with me through my sister's dream.

I gave birth to my daughter before my son turned two. My husband and I were delighted. We could finally name her Foz — short for Foziya. Whenever I called my daughter's name, I felt my aunt's presence.

While I was pregnant with my second daughter, my friend asked me, "Why don't you name her Fay? You already have Foz. Both names would be cute together." I considered the name, but I was still in doubt. My mom told her sister that I was thinking of calling my daughter Fay. To my surprise, my aunt dreamt her sister, Aunt Foziya, asked why I was hesitant. In Arabic, Fay meant shade; a word that symbolized what she provided for us when she was alive – she was the shade of our family. The answer was in my tears. I decided to name my second daughter Fay. I was truly blessed that all my children carried a piece of my dear aunt with them. My son wore her bracelet and my daughters shared her name.

When I catch a glimpse of the comedy I watched the night she died, a melancholic cloud wraps itself around me, but soon it condenses into sweet raindrops, showering me with blessings. The comedy reminds me of her sense of humor, which paints the brightest smiles on my face. Her lively "visits" made her play a significant and endless role in my life. My aunt was with me all along. She never left.

FAITH

By Carolyn T. Johnson

In Honor of Mrs. Anna Rado

At eighty years of age, a head full of gray hair and an angelic smile on her face, Anna took her place behind the podium, looked out at the audience, clasped her hands, took a deep breath, and began to tell her story of…

….being forced from her home into a ghetto, then crammed into cattle cars for deportation from Hungary to Auschwitz at the tender age of thirteen

…..standing for selection, with her family, in front of Mengele, and seeing her mother and father for the last time before they were ordered left, to the gas chambers, while she and her older sister were sent to the right, to barracks

…..her sister taken to a different labor camp, while she was thrown into a barrack full of children, where a clandestine bathroom conversation with a benevolent German woman advised her to say she was not thirteen, but sixteen, she could work, be useful

…..hiding when the SS guards took a group of sixteen year old girls away to a wooden-floored room, then shot them in the head, to listen to the sound of their dead bodies hitting the floor

…..standing for selection again in front of Mengele, stripped naked, covered in lice bites and being sent to the left to be gassed, yet given an overcoat by a kind German woman and told to sneak back into the line on the right, for survivors

….liberated by the Russians and walking for six days, past bombed-out bridges and devastation to go home, to Hungary, to find her family

….held under Communist rule in Hungary for eleven years and being captured by the KGB and jailed in a thwarted attempt to escape with her brother and his family

…..sharing a home with another family, marrying their son and giving birth to her two children, before the Hungarian borders finally opened, allowing them to flee to the United States to join her older sister

.....now talking to schoolchildren and adults alike, telling them of her stolen childhood, her time in Auschwitz, putting it in terms they could understand, of teaching them how to see themselves in a stranger's eyes .....answering my only question, of how she could still believe in a God that would let this kind of thing happen, and, with tears welling up in her kind eyes, she stated simply, "Because they were bad people, he is not a bad God."

FAMILY BLESSINGS
By Paula Timpson

The Family
Is the heart of Love
Together
Always in spirit and hope
Miracle is
A family
Close as blades of grass growing
Or the wind touching kites flying high
Believe
Begin
Be open to receiving and giving love
Family blessings

THERE FOREVER
By Elynne Chaplik-Aleskow

We had long talks while sharing a paddle boat on the lake near both our apartments in Chicago's Lincoln Park. My friend was decades older than I which gifted me her wisdom and extraordinary insights and perceptions. Our talks in that boat taught me life lessons I will carry with me until the day I die.

One Sunday as we drifted on the pond talking and enjoying each other's thoughts, my friend suddenly said: "When I die, I hope to come back as a seagull."

"Why a seagull?" I asked.

I smiled as I watched my dear friend staring at the seagulls flying over the glistening water.

"They are graceful and free. That is my hope."

It was very painful for me when my friend retired and moved to another state. Visiting her was not the same as sharing time with her on a regular basis in Chicago. We had to rely on the phone and e-mails to stay in touch. Our connection and understanding of one another were so strong that our discussions never lost their depth or truth.

I will never forget the e-mail I opened that day:

And now the truth about me and all. I have lung cancer. Termination date two months. I am writing this because I cannot talk very well and get so breathless. I have hospice coming the last week and they have been superb. As of yesterday I took to bed because I am so weak. Other than weakness, I have no pain. Since January I have suspected that something was wrong. I am relieved to know the truth. I am ready in all ways to join my energy with outer space. The body has become rusty--- eyes, ears, joints, and lungs. It is my time and I am completely at one with nature. So be with me and experience the relief from all troubles I have. I will always be with you in spirit. Love to you always. Your devoted friend.

I was stunned. I started to cry and could not stop.

She was able to send me more e-mails during the time she was dying. I cherished every word she used her strength to share and always

14

replied with the gratitude that my beloved friend was still able to receive my notes. I was even able to briefly speak to her by phone although her energy was almost gone.

And then the last e-mail came:

This may be the last letter I can send. I am not supposed to exert too much energy. I have no pain but no appetite, no energy, and sleep most of the time. The end will come soon – I hope. I know that this is a difficult time for you, and my heart goes out to you. The spirit is a strong bond and will be there forever. Love always.

Over and over I re-read these last e-mails and all the cards and notes I had received from her over the years of our friendship. Her written words were priceless and helped me to feel close to her.

Several weeks after my friend died, I took a walk along the lake where we had always gone to talk. I was profoundly sad and longed to speak with her, wishing for a sign from her. As I stood lost in my thoughts while looking at the water, I suddenly felt a presence near me. I slowly turned my head and looked down. There next to me was a beautiful seagull. It was looking up at me. Neither of us moved for quite a while. I felt a calm within me. Then, I smiled, and the seagull flew away to freedom.

"Miracles occur naturally as expressions of love.
The real miracle is the love that inspires them.
In this sense everything that comes from love is a miracle."
~ - Marianne Williamson

A MIRACLE
By Louise Borad Gerber

Though you no longer live
nightly I beckon your images,
the ones that watch over me
as I slumber.
"Visit me my daughter,
 Let me see you,
let me hear you."

Last night
a strange sound attracted my attention.
Searching for the source
I finally found a tape recorder,
long ago shelved and forgotten.

Turning it off I wondered
how long it had been running.
Rewinding the tape
I heard your voice and mine,
exchanging our repartee,
so often repeated.

The tape ends with your words,
"I love my momma."
and me saying,
"Thank you for the kiss."

16

HEROES
By Terri Elders

Nearly a year had gone by since Ken died. As the anniversary of that sad day neared, I felt lonely and longed for a chat. I wanted to tell him that the neighbors across the way finally painted their house, that I didn't like the current contestants on *American Idol*, and that his favorite restaurant had slated a lobster fest. Most of all, I just wanted to hear his voice.

Then one morning as I dusted the den, I paused as I slid the cloth around the frame of one of his favorite lithographs, the one hanging on the wall above his overstuffed chair. The sepia-toned collage featured portraits of two dozen movie buckaroos, ranging from Johnny Mack Brown to John Wayne. Its caption, "All of My Hero's Are Cowboys," had made me grin when he'd first positioned the picture when we moved into our retirement home.

"It's tough to make two mistakes in one word," I'd said, "but the artist managed. He's got a superfluous apostrophe and a misspelled plural. It should be h-e-r-o-e-s."

Ken laughed. "I'd never noticed before. I've had this for years, but I've always been too busy admiring those actors. I love Westerns because the good guys always win."

Ken claimed his mom had named him for one of the Western stars in the painting, Ken Maynard. "I'm just glad he was the one she idolized, rather than a couple of the other guys up there. I can't imagine having gone through life as Hoot or Hopalong."

I looked at the lithograph more closely. "Hmmm. There's also Lash Larue and Crash Corrigan here. Lash or Crash would have been dashing."

"I'll settle for plain old Ken."

Ken once bragged that he must have seen a hundred Westerns by the time he hit third grade. His mom dropped him off at the theater every Saturday afternoon for the double features. During the summers while she worked he'd go three or four times a week. He listened to *The*

Lone Ranger and *The Cisco Kid* on the radio and later watched every Western series that appeared on television.

The only song he claimed to know the lyrics to was "Paladin," the theme tune from *Have Gun – Will Travel*, a late '50s TV show later adapted to radio. Whenever that show appeared on one of the many cable channels Ken subscribed to during his last years, he'd record each episode and watch them over and over.

"He's a true hero," Ken explained. "Many of the movie cowboys jump right into a fight, but Paladin first tried to settle disputes without violence whenever he possibly could. He not only had brains, he had class. He loved good food, good wine and sharp clothes."

Just like my husband, I'd thought to myself, a man who served up even simple grilled burgers gorgeously garnished, who routinely sniffed and swirled his favorite chenin blanc before sipping, and who insisted on ironing his own shirts to get the collars and cuffs just right.

"Here's the thing about Westerns," he'd explained, after watching an episode of *Cheyenne* just days before he died. "Life's uncertain enough just as it is. You don't need any ambiguity in your entertainment. So many of the new movies you watch leave too many questions unanswered. I want everything crystal clear at the end. I want to believe that justice always will out."

My gallant and gutsy husband had absorbed his diagnosis of pancreatic cancer with what seemed to me an almost heroic grace. As he steadily declined during those last months, he rarely complained and never whimpered.

"I can't tell you how brave I think you are," I'd say.

"Brave? Nah. Just accepting the inevitable," he answered. "Tom Mix wouldn't be boohooing. Neither would Wild Bill Elliott."

Ken tried to be a good guy until the end, I now recalled, finishing the dusting. He died in discomfort, yes, but without experiencing the pain that so many with a similar diagnosis have had to endure. He chalked it up to karma.

After I finished tidying the den, I decided I'd settle down to watch a video. I rummaged through some of Ken's old DVDs, and paused at one titled *50 Western Classics.*

Then I heard Ken whisper, just as clearly as if he'd been standing in the room next to me: "Did you get a birthday card for Rick?"

I glanced around and of course there was nobody else in the room. Yet I was convinced it had been his voice…his soft inflection, his wry tone.

"Oh, heavens," I thought. "He's right!" I realized I'd forgotten Ken's middle son's birthday which was coming up fast. I closed the entertainment center's cabinet door. Instead of watching a DVD, I'd drive to town and get a card. Then I'd stop by the post office for some stamps so I could mail it.

As I entered the post office, I glanced at the display case. The new commemorative stamps, "Cowboys of the Silver Screen," bore portraits of four of the men in Ken's lithograph: William S. Hart, Tom Mix, Gene Autry, and Roy Rogers. All four wore jaunty white cowboy hats. I could almost hear Ken's voice again, reminding me that anybody could tell they were all good guys.

I twisted my mouth into a smile as I approached the counter, even though I had to stifle a sniffle.

"I'll take five sheets of the cowboy stamps," I said, reaching into my purse for a tissue. I blotted a tear from my eye.

The post office worker opened her drawer and counted out several sheets. "Got a spring allergy?" she asked.

"Nope. I'm just overjoyed by these stamps."

"Well, they're certainly cheery," she said, totaling my tab.

"They remind me so much of my husband."

"Whatever." She shrugged and reached for my credit card. She glanced from the stamps to my face and back, and then shook her head.

I ducked my head to hide a smirk. She thinks I'm the odd one, I thought. I bet she doesn't know that Paladin's horse was named Tanglefoot or that Tom Mix's was Tony. I bet she thinks Cheyenne is just a city in Wyoming!

A couple of days later I dropped in at the post office again, thinking I'd purchase some additional sheets of that stamp. They'd be handy for sending Christmas and birthday cards to Ken's other friends and family.

"They're sold out already," the postal clerk said. "They went the first day we got them.

Later I checked online at the United States Postal Service website. They were all gone there, too. If I hadn't thought I heard Ken's voice, I never would have gone to town that day nor had a chance to buy those stamps.

Whether it came from inside or outside of my head…that whispered reminder about Rick's card reassured me that my husband still cared about me. He'd found a way to steer me away from melancholy into happy memories. Long after he'd ridden into his final sunset, Ken still knew how to be a good guy, a hero. I call that a miracle indeed.

MAN ALIVE
By Cherise Wyneken

Tall Banyan trees
canopy the playground
where children swing and climb.
Push me, Daddy, Billy cries.

Phil's friend rides up
in a brand new three-speed bike.
Take a look, Phil says to Dad.
My birthday's coming soon.

Hey, Pops. Can I use the car tonight?
Can you spare some change for gas?
Will you help me with this math?

He lies there
plugged into machines
his life fast going out.
Please, Father. Make him well again.

Push, bike, car, change, help,

MAN ALIVE

Sometimes Fathers give us what we ask for
just because we ask.

THE EAGLE HAS LANDED
By Edward Louis

"The Eagle has landed," I said confidently into the lobby telephone of a quiet Rio de Janeiro hotel. As I hung up, the desk clerk looked at me oddly.

"Just calling my wife," I nodded and began dragging my suitcase towards the elevator.

It was my safe arrival call back home – the importance of which had been drilled into me by my father as I was growing up.

It seemed I couldn't leave our property without hearing him bellow, "Call me when you get there." His desire to protect us was ever-present. "Watch where you're going" or "be careful with that" tripped off his tongue as easily as "hello."

As I grew up, got married, and started my own family, I began to understand his need to know that nothing had harmed us when we were away from him. Life was good, but my job required me to do a lot of international traveling. Long flights, busy meetings, and hotel rooms in foreign countries meant little time for me to watch over my family – or for my family to watch over me.

Before the advent of cell phones and email, personal communication from these locales was often inconvenient and always expensive. Instead of having a long telephone conversation relaying the day's events, a brief "safe arrival" call would have to suffice. I would call my wife, Wendy, and recite the famous words said by Neil Armstrong in 1969 during the Apollo 11 moon landing: "The Eagle has landed." With that simple phrase, she would know that I had gotten to my destination as planned and everything was okay.

As our kids grew up and moved away, she, too, would have her share of exotic travels – like to California to see our daughter or to Florida to visit our sons. No matter where she went, I could be assured of a safe arrival call with our signature phrase.

Over the years, we discussed the last trip either one of us would ever have to take – that trip to the "Great Beyond." We always said that the one who got there first needed to send back a sign that they had crossed over successfully – in essence, giving a "safe arrival" call.

More than 30 years later – and eight months after being diagnosed with pancreatic cancer – my wife took that final trip. The thought of any kind of sign was the furthest thing from my mind. But on the morning of her funeral, my sister and I spotted an eagle flying over our house.

It might not have been such a big deal if eagles were commonly seen in my area, but they aren't. It was the first – and last – time I had ever seen one in several years of living there. My next door neighbor, who is an avid bird watcher, also saw the eagle that morning and confirmed it was a rare sighting.

The eagle circled our home and perched itself in a large tree on our property. It stared down at us for the longest time – almost as if it wanted to make sure we saw it. "It's Wendy," my sister announced as we stared back at the eagle.

Tears began to fill my eyes as we watched it finally fly away. "I think you're right. It's her sign to us: the Eagle has landed."

Previously published in *Hope Whispers* (Whispering Angel Books)

What if you gave someone a gift, and they neglected to thank you for it - would you be likely to give them another? Life is the same way. In order to attract more of the blessings that life has to offer, you must truly appreciate what you already have. ~ Ralph Marston

YOU ARE MY HERO
By Lynn C. Johnston

You lead by your example
You find strength where there was none
You stand by all that you believe
And you stay when most would run
You march to your own drummer
And you're faithful to your heart
You've made the hard decisions
That would tear the rest of us apart
You could've crumbled from the pressure
When life broke your heart in two
Instead you fought with all your might
Until your skies returned to blue
A modest soul you'll always have
Without your accolades in tow
You claim you're nothing special
But you're wrong; you are my hero
You struggle like we all do
Through this experience called life
Yet your grace and your tenacity
Inspire me to rise above the strife
Like a Phoenix you have risen
From the ashes and the flames
You've stood up even when
You had to take the blame
Your life has not been easy
But somehow you've made it through
You'll always be my hero
And I'm awfully proud of you

Previously published in *Angel's Dance: A Collection of Uplifting & Inspirational Poetry* (Whispering Angel Books)

NEXT DOOR ANGEL
By Debbie Acklin

It was summer and I was twelve. My friend and I had been walking the neighborhood at dusk because it was the coolest time to be outside. We were doing what twelve-year-old girls do, chatting, singing, being silly, and just enjoying one another's company.

On this particular night, we got this eerie feeling that we were being watched. It's odd how that happens, but we both felt it. About a block from our street, not wanting to appear afraid, we kept our pace steady, not hurrying.

"We should be back on our street in a few minutes," I said. "Yes, our brothers are still outside, riding their bikes," said my friend. This was our way of communicating to our potential watcher that we were safer than we might look.

The next night, while her parents were out, someone tried to break into a bathroom window of my friend's house. Her two older brothers frightened him away.

I saw the lights from the police car when they pulled up down the street, but I didn't learn what had happened until the next day. "Do you think this was the person watching us yesterday?" I asked. "I bet it was," she whispered. "Someone was watching to see when the car was gone before they tried to break in," she guessed.

This man may or may not have been the person who was watching us. In fact we had no proof that anyone was watching us at all, just a gut feeling. Still I feared that he would try to come for me next.

We had many discussions about it over the next week. This was high drama for twelve year olds. We were not afraid during the day. It was the nights that we feared. Well, I feared them. She had a house full of people at all times. I had two younger brothers and a mom. My dad was in Vietnam.

We did not have central air, just a window unit in the kitchen. At night, unless it was abnormally hot, we turned it off and opened the windows. I began to keep my windows closed and locked, my curtains pulled. I also pulled the covers up to my chin, a ridiculous safety ploy, but one every child understands. I would lie there, unable to sleep, imagining that someone was watching and waiting.

When I did fall asleep, I would wake up several times a night, usually sweating heavily from the closed windows, the covers, and the fear. I remember reciting a kind of rhyming prayer that I had learned as a very small child, "Four corners to my bed. Four angels 'round my head. One to keep me. One to pray. Two to guide me through each day." I did not want to close my eyes, but fatigue always won out.

One evening, my brothers, my mom and I went to visit with a family down the street. We enjoyed a meal and then played pinochle for a while. Having not slept much, I was the first to grow tired and decided to go ahead and walk home.

It wasn't long before I noticed that a car was following me down the street. I was right on the curb and the car was not passing. It was keeping pace with me. I didn't want to go back since that was the direction of the car, and I didn't want to run, yet. When I arrived at the bottom of my driveway, I was sure they would continue on. I was wrong. The car followed me up the driveway. As I approached the front door, I heard a car door open and shut behind me.

In our neighborhood, doors were seldom locked unless everyone was settled in for the night. We had been gone and ours were not locked. All of our lights were off. The house, inside and outside, was totally dark. Part of me was afraid to enter the house; part of me felt an urgency to do so, quickly.

About that time, our next door neighbor, a Green Beret, came pulling into his driveway on his motorcycle. It was impossible not to notice him since his motorcycle was pretty loud. He pulled his beret on as he hopped off his bike and waved.

I guess the sight of him was too risky. I heard the car door open and shut again. I turned just in time to see a dark car pulling out of my driveway. Thankfully, I also saw the rest of my family making their way down the street toward home. I waited on the front porch so we could enter the house together.

"Who was that in the driveway?" my mother asked me. "I don't know," I replied, "but they followed me home. "

"I don't think so, honey. Why would they follow you?" she asked. "They were probably just at the wrong house."

I told her the whole story. The feeling someone was watching us, our take on the break in down the street, and now this. It was clear that she thought I was letting my imagination run wild.

I added. "Mr. M. pulled up on his motorcycle and scared them away."

My mom gave me the strangest look. "You know that Mr. M. is in Vietnam with daddy," she said. Yes, I did know that, but I was so relieved to see him pull into his driveway that I forgotten. "He must be back," I said, "He even waved to me."

"No, honey, he's not back." I was not convinced. I had seen him. My mother had to walk me next door to talk with his wife who confirmed that he was still overseas.

That night, after praying and repeating my angel rhyme in my head, I thought about Mr. M. He was there. I saw him and I heard his motorcycle and so did the person who was following me. Suddenly, I noticed a light at the end of my bed. At first I thought it was a trick of the eye, the angle of the street light through my curtains. I just lay still and watched it, wondering. I began to feel a sense of calm slowly flow through me.

I knew, just as sure as I knew anything in this world, that I was being visited by an angel. God had sent this messenger to me to let me know He was watching over me. Maybe this had been who I had mistaken for Mr. M.

All my fear dissipated. I tossed the covers off of me and got up and opened the windows to the small, but welcome, breeze. Back in bed, I looked at the foot of my bed. The light was still there, a soft glowing shape. It was the best night's sleep I had it days. No other incidents disturbed those carefree summer days.

Previously published in *Chicken Soup for the Soup: Angels Among Us*
(Chicken Soup for the Soul Publishing, LLC)

"Miracles never cease to amaze me. I expect them, but their consistent arrival is always delightful to experience". ~ Mark Victor Hansen

GENERATIONS/PHOTOGRAPH
By Juley Harvey

my mother gave me a photograph
of four generations of women
in the family.
it speaks sweetly
in strong, golden, sepia tones,
of a forged strength,
and gives me a palpable
feeling of strength passing
through their linked lives, their fingers,
all fragrant with green-bean-stringing,
and roll-baking and life-molding,
to mine.
it tells me
i will endure,
to shape and love
and create with my own hands
the things that have come down
through theirs,
in a recycling of precious materials.
a photograph, like a generation,
changes and remains the same,
shapes, molds,
reshapes,
sharpens, softens,
ages, youths,
remembers, forgets,
botoxes, lines,
speaks, is silent,
disappears, stays,
fogs, brightens,
breathes, moves, stills,

follows us, as history,
present, future days
unwind, rewind,
hots and chills, spills, thrills,
imperfect imperfections,
radiance, earthiness,
glows, glowers,
sunspots, liver spots,
centers, pinking-sheared edges,
the dough of life, flakiness,
sustaining, rising,
rising, rising,
big, faraway,
before my eyes.
they dot my eyes, i's.
picture this —
"we" melts down
to "me,"
starring in my own mystery,
directed by the unseen
quiet silver queens of history,
even as we look upon it.
were we ever that way,
we are left to wonder.
memory is strong;
strong women more so.
their power cannot be reproduced
in the chemistry of even the
kindest male,
for it lies in the continuity,
serenity, and eternity linked
in the hands of female generations,
forged by the fires of gentle persuasions.
a light passed on from life to life,
my i is sum they.
i take their torch to find the way.

ALL I HAD TO DO WAS ASK
By Linda Lohman

It had been three years since the loss of my husband. To others it was cancer; to me, it was a heart-ectomy.

Vern was a perfectionist that made jewelry. Prior to his last hospitalization, I had lost a pearl out of a ring. He said as soon as he could, he would get a matched pearl to repair it. The problem was that he never came out of the hospital. He never got well enough to shop for a pearl. And he did not tell me where he had put the ring. I had torn the house apart looking for it. My sister, Marilyn, had helped me search. We checked the linings of the drapes, his jackets, and everywhere we thought he might have put it before going into the hospital the last time. We had finally given up.

I thought I was getting on with my life. I had been dating. I had made new friends that were older and single, like me. I had joined Toastmasters. I won a club award for MOST INSPIRATIONAL SPEAKER.

But I knew I was a fraud when I went to hang that award on the wall in the hall leading to the master bedroom. A bedroom I had not entered for three years. How could I be inspirational when I couldn't even sleep in my own bedroom?

After Vern passed, I moved into a smaller bedroom off the kitchen. I moved my clothes from the master bedroom into the closet of that room. My life changed. I missed him just as much every single day. But I was learning to live with that loss as one learns to live with the amputation of a limb. The living part was getting easier. The loss part was never easier.

There truly is no loss in the world comparable to the loss of a spouse. I know I cried buckets! But it was time to restock my emotional self.

And restock is what I did when I looked down the hall at that closed bedroom door. In a demon-like frenzy, I threw open the door and dusted the furniture. I changed the bed sheets and began moving my clothes into the closet. And I prayed.

With each step I took I asked God for strength and a sign I was moving in the right direction. I was gaining strength even in small steps. Then I realized this was the "growth" that was talked about. This was the "growing through grief" that I needed. But I still wanted a sign.

I remember the day my garage door wouldn't open. I had learned to open it manually. It felt like a nuisance that made me late for an appointment. Within a few days, the electricity went off. Guess what? I did not panic. I already knew how to get the door open. The day that happened, I knew that God was teaching me lesson after lesson every day of my life. I needed to be awake and alert enough to learn from them.

Today I was opening myself up to another lesson. I was cleaning the bathroom in the master bedroom when it happened. I was throwing out all the pills that were in the medicine cabinet and flushing them down the toilet. I opened a small container which would contain my allergy medication and saw my Mikimoto pearl ring. The ring missing since before Vern passed away.

Finding the ring was the sign I was doing the right thing. Tearfully I called my sister. I explained that I was moving back into the bedroom. She heard my tears and immediately suggested maybe this was too soon.

"No, Sis. It's not too soon. You will never guess what I just found." I sobbed.

"What?"

"The pearl ring."

"NO WAY! We searched that room from top to bottom." She replied.

"And you will never guess. Remember the pearl that was missing? The one I wanted Vern to match?"

"Yes." She said.

"Well, the ring is perfect. No pearls are missing. They are all there. I can't even remember which one was missing. But they are ALL there now."

My grief was not eased at once by moving back into the master bedroom. But I slept that night knowing The Teacher above was continuing to provide life lessons with every step I took. All I had to do was ASK.

YOU MAKE ME SMILE
By Lynn C. Johnston

In a world that can get crazy
Where values often go astray
It's easy to forget what counts
As we struggle through each day

But sometimes on the road of life
You get to meet someone who cares
Who remembers what does matter most
The love and laughter that they share

They know nothing's more important
Than the love that's left behind
Making someone feel they're cherished
Building loving ties that bind

All their special loved ones
Reside deep within their heart
Yet they always share the pieces
So everyone can have a part

You are that special someone
Who only comes once in a while
And I feel blessed to know you
Because you make me smile

Previously published in *Angel's Dance: A Collection of Uplifting & Inspirational Poetry* (Whispering Angel Books)

SNOW ANGELS
By Rosemary McKinley

All too often, we think that people today are cold and insensitive when it comes to strangers. I must confess I agreed with that sentiment until something happened to change this doubting Thomas.

In December of 2009 on a Sunday, we had a blizzard with about 18-inches of snow predicted. I was caring for my dad this particular weekend. We took all the precautions; we had the snow shovel ready and plenty of food in the house. My dad is blind, only able to see shadows, and is on oxygen all of the time.

I had just made us lunch and we were chatting in the living room. Then I decided to take a nap so that I would be ready to shovel in a few hours.

While I was resting, my dad went out the front door to look at the snow. Our front door automatically locks when it closes, so he was locked out. But since we usually leave the back door unlocked, he did not call out to me thinking he could walk around to the back and let himself in. He underestimated the height of the snow and ended up in the street.

When I woke up from my nap after about twenty minutes, I couldn't find him. I walked into every room calling his name but he wasn't there. In a rush to find him, I grabbed my coat and boots and ran outside. I still couldn't find him for a few minutes. I was frantic calling him and then screaming his name.

Finally I saw this figure lying in the road on the snow. I ran over to him and kept calling his name. He was unconscious but came to after a few minutes. Then I was even more frantic because I wasn't able to help him stand. He had no coat on and he was shivering. The snow was high, about a foot at that point. I started to yell, "Help, help!" There was no one around because of the snow and it was still falling. We were so close to the house and yet so far because he couldn't walk without his oxygen.

I had to make a decision and make it fast, either leave him in the snow on the street or keep trying to get him back into the house. I had left my cell phone in the house in my haste to run outside. If I had it, I could have called 911 for help.

All alone on the road, I kept yelling for help hoping someone would hear me. Then something short of a miracle happened. An SUV appeared as if from nowhere. The passenger window rolled down and a woman said, "Can we help?"

"Yes," I replied. "Could you call 911?"

Two women got out of her vehicle with blankets. We placed one under my father and one on top of him. The women stayed with me until help arrived.

"Thank you so much. By the way how are you out on such a bad day?"

The woman replied, "Normally we are delivering the Sunday news early in the morning about 6:00 AM, but the roads were impassible this morning. That's why we are here now.

"Lucky for us, thanks again, you saved my father today".

Within a short time a policeman came to the rescue and he asked, "What do you want me to do?"

My dad piped up and said, "No ambulance."

The policeman looked at me and said, "We can't take him against his will."

Then I said, "Can you help me get him into the house?"

The policeman and I managed to get my dad back into the house. I helped him remove his wet clothes. He suggested getting under the covers and sleeping. I piled comforter upon blanket on him as he slept. After a few hours, he seemed much better and warmer. He ate dinner and he laughingly said, "The blankets were too heavy; I couldn't move."

I knew that he was fine after his sense of humor came back. Between the policeman and the two angels who happened to be in the right place for us that afternoon, I felt blessed.

I never saw those two women again and I don't know for sure if they were angels but the timing was too perfect. I did not see one newspaper in the car, nor were they delivering them as they were leaving.

ODE TO THE RESCUERS
By Quilliam Horace Flint

In too many ways life is a dried windblown path of dust
That those who are downtrodden tread because they must.
That path stretches out for miles on end,
So lonely and cold to wander without a friend.
Without a companion to walk by our side,
Helping to steady us and serve as our guide,
We dogs are lost and become quite glum,
Chased away by many who label us dumb.
That path then becomes a minefield of danger,
Making us wary to approach any stranger.
But there are those who make strides in winning our hearts,
Who persist and press on to help find us new starts.
When finally embraced by a rescuer kind,
We find there are flowers where once there were mines.
In a world that is often too cold and too bleak,
There are those who for us choose loudly to speak
And because they strive every day and each night,
Our hearts that were heavy now are made to feel light.
We thank you deeply for all that you do,
Well aware that the path has been hard for you too.
And we want you to know that the tears which you cry
Will moisten the earth that before seemed so dry.
And with the softness that now your tears do yield,
Will come in our hearts a blossoming flower field.
So please never doubt that your efforts are golden
And that for you we animals are certainly beholden.

THE BURMESE SHIRT
By Theresa Peipins

After living abroad in Barcelona, Spain for twenty years, a series of major life changes brought me back to the city where I had lived many years before, Buffalo, New York. When I arrived in Buffalo, I put a copy of a *New Yorker* cartoon on my bulletin board. The cartoon shows two women seated in front of a fireplace. One says, "I'm burning all my little black dresses and moving upstate." It summed up how I imagined my life would be back in this post-industrial city.

Nothing could be further from the truth. After years of living in a densely populated vibrant city, I settled into a beautiful peaceful city and I found a job in my profession (ESL educator) teaching refugees and immigrants. I had been teaching in universities for most of my career but now found myself in adult education which gave me a sense of providing a useful service to people who truly needed the skills I could offer. And I certainly learned a great deal from my students about how to adapt to dramatic changes and live with a generous heart and spirit.

This job also brought me back full circle to my own life. My parents arrived as Latvian refugees after World War ll and met each other in Buffalo. Today, the refugees are from different countries but their stories are similar and that leads me to the shirt that has changed my life.

I received a gift from the mother of a Karenni student in my class. The Karenni are an ethnic and cultural population in Burma. They have been fighting the Burmese government for decades for recognition of their basic rights and many have spent years in refugee camps on the Thai border. The shirt is immediately recognizable by anyone in that community or from Burma. It has the typical embroidery and fringe that make it distinctive. Mine is black (certain colors are for women) with red, pink, blue, yellow and white cross stitching across the chest. Two red strings dangle from the neckline and red fringe is on the bottom. The fringe swings gently as I move across a room. This garment has the beauty of a handmade creation and has an elegance and simplicity to its design.

This shirt has become my default piece of wardrobe for any special event. I wear it to openings, readings, parties, and of course, Burmese festivities. I wear it as the Karenni do, to mark special occasions. Most recently I wore it on the occasion of the 75th birthday of a dear friend. This shirt has symbolized what my new life here has come to mean. Every time I put on the shirt, I am connected to the world in a broader sense and my small part in it. The shirt reminds me of the struggles of so many people around the world. It reminds me of the sacrifices my own parents made to give me an opportunity to be able to live my own privileged life and, most of all, it gives me pleasure in its beauty.

*"When I started counting my blessings,
my whole life turned around."* ~Willie Nelson

WITHOUT A DOUBT
By Vanessa A. Jackson Austin

As I am faced with doubt,
God whispers, *"Trust Me,
I will bring you out."*

As I encounter life's raging storms,
God whispers, *"I got this;
Stay calm."*

As I cry out,
"Lord, help me, please!"
God whispers, *"I will fight
Your treacherous disease."*

Previously published in *Cries in the Wind* (WestBow Press)

THE GRATEFUL GOODBYE
By Carolyn T. Johnson

I took one last deep breath, exhaled, and grabbed the handle of the big wooden door. The foyer of the funeral parlor, crowded with family and friends from the small town my grandmother called home, looked like a sea of black. Boxes of tissue dotted the tops of end tables. A pungent floral scent assaulted my nostrils. Air conditioning, blasting from the vent overhead, sent a chill up my spine.

In my 35 years, I had never experienced a family member or a close friend pass away. The whole idea of viewings, funerals, and gravesites tied my stomach up in knots. And for the first one to be my grandmother's, the woman whose phone number I knew by heart from calling it so often, was overwhelming.

Aunt Sandra broke my train of thought. "Sugar, I'm so glad you're finally here. Your daddy's been asking about you. It's all such a shock, her dying so sudden." She dabbed at her teary eyes and took my hand. "But she sure looks pretty in her yellow Sunday best. Come on. I'll take you to her."

"No way. I'm not going in there."

"But Honey, she'd want you to."

"Aunt Sandra, I'm sorry, but, I'm not going to have the last memories of Maamaw be her lying dead in a box."

"It's not like that. She looks peaceful. And you don't want to regret not saying your final goodbyes."

"Well, I don't care. I want to remember her among the living." I burst out in tears, extracted my hand from Aunt Sandra's and got lost in the crowd.

The next day, the funeral took place in a standing-room-only Baptist Church. I sat with my family in the same front pew I used to sit in when I'd spend summers at Maamaw's house. I didn't remember much of what was said. It was hard to concentrate with that mahogany casket staring me in the face.

We moved on to the graveside at the only cemetery in town. It was covered in a big green tent with a matching cloth draped over a mound of dirt and white chairs blanketed in green velvet were set out for family. Rather than focusing on the disturbing thought of my grandmother's lifeless body being laid to rest, I, now dazed and emotionally spent, made it through the brief service by admiring the beautiful sprays of roses surrounding the open grave. Maamaw's favorite red roses cascaded along the top of the casket, while rainbows of roses adorned the other arrangements.

When the service finally drew to an end, I stood motionless and watched, eyes wide in disbelief, as family and friends plucked roses from the top of the coffin.

"Here's a rose to remember your grandmother by," said Dad.

"I don't want it. It belongs to her. Not me," I blubbered.

"Darling daughter, roses should be for the living."

"I don't care. I'll see you back at the house," and with that I turned and walked the three blocks to Maamaw's house.

The mood back at the house was semi-somber. People looked more at ease. I listened as they recalled some familiar, some new stories of my grandmother's 77 years on this earth.

After an hour of glad-handing, I slipped off and made the short walk back to the cemetery. Gone were the green tent and chairs, but what astounded me were the barren sprays. Not a rose in sight.

I lingered over the freshly strewn dirt, tearfully saying my last goodbyes to the woman who loved me best. "At the time, I thought it was awful, people taking your roses, from the top of your casket even, but now that they're all gone, I kind of wish I had one to press in the bible you gave me."

And at the instant, out of the cloudless, sunlit sky, came a short gust of wind, knocking over three of the sprays.

I picked up the sprays, one-by-one, repositioning the prongs firmly into the ground. When I got to the third one, a small spot of red caught my eye on the neighboring spray. One last red rose, previously covered by the fallen sprays, peeked its head out. A smile reached my lips as I gently plucked it from the surrounding greenery, clutched it to my breast, looked towards the heavens and blew my grandmother a grateful kiss.

EVERYTHING ELSE
By Lynn Pinkerton

By the time I came to know him, he was a wizened old gnome of a man. Crunched and crippled. A long way from his mother's early cradling. From the tenderly chosen name she gave him when he was bright new. I sometimes wondered if his soft, tiny baby legs kicked out long and free or if from the get-go they hunkered down, squashed and bent, resulting in the insect imitation that earned him his nickname, "Grasshopper."

He arrived in my life one hot summer morning when I was twelve. Maybe thirteen. Arrived in the back of a pick-up truck driven by my dad. I watched with fascination as the tail-gate clanked down and my dad lifted him out and gently set him down in the front yard. I wondered why he didn't stand up. Why he just squatted there, bony knees flung out to each side like spiky antennae. He seemed to search the horizon for what he couldn't see from his low vantage point.

My dad called me over, made introductions, and explained that Grasshopper would be doing some yard work and he would be back later to take him home. As my dad drove off, Grasshopper nodded at me and slowly began making his way to the edge of the flower bed. Using his signature means of locomotion, he propelled himself along by substituting conscripted arms for legs. Time after time, gloved fists pushed his body off the ground as he swung himself forward. Again and again it went until he got where he was going. Then he set about diligently pulling pesky weeds, clipping grass along the edge and deadheading my dad's favorite roses.

He came often the next several years. As a youngster, I sometimes thought it would make more sense for my dad to help out by just giving him money. It didn't seem fair that Grasshopper should have to creep around our yard pulling up crab grass to earn money for bread and bologna. Of course, I now know he and my dad had some sort of tacit agreement. My dad understood Grasshopper's need to know the dignity of a job. Of being self-sufficient. And Grasshopper felt pride in being offered honest work.

It was a mystery to me that Grasshopper seemed to have made a sort of patient peace with his life and circumstance. His watery old eyes held a twinkle and I would often catch him chanting a little tune or humming. Sometimes my Mom would have me fill a Mason jar with ice water and take it out to him. Always grateful, he would take a short break, wipe away the streaming sweat, and ask how I was doing. One day my younger brother followed me outside and stood by, sheepishly digging one toe into the crunchy summer grass. He finally looked down at Grasshopper and in a small voice offered, "Mr. Grasshopper, I'm sorry about your broken legs."

An easy, sweet smile sprawled across Grasshopper's pecan-colored face. "Don't you worry none 'bout these legs, Honey Chile. Everything else I got works just fine."

"A gentle word, a kind look, a good-natured smile can work wonders and accomplish miracles." ~ William Hazlitt

HEAL
By Paula Timpson

Animals heal us
Every day
Simply
Knowing to lay nearby in silence
Touching us with their furry bodies
Making us
Better
Because of their love
Animals trust the way
They don't have any questions
In the moment they present themselves
To the Spirit and they rise
refreshing us all anew

JOURNEY GENTLERS
By Beckie A. Miller

*"Hope is the thing with feathers, that perches in the soul,
and sings the tune without words and never stops at all..." ~Emily Dickinson*

Nothing raises the spirits more, brings tears to tender hearts, or provides us with cathartic hope than a miracle or special blessing does. I was raised with an old-fashioned Catholic upbringing and as a result I truly believe in miracles. As a child, I remember often being frustrated because I prayed for miracles and too often nothing happened, at least in my childlike worldview. In all fairness though, what a child deems a miracle is sometimes a lot more trivial than what an adult considers one to be. If all of us, however, can always believe with childlike innocence no matter what comes our way, we will be blessed with enough miracles and blessings to sustain us through the toughest journeys in life.

I grew into an adult with much life experience that some might call aging, not me however! As I have "matured," I have come to believe the only difference between miracles and blessings is the size and scope. Some miracles can be considered so because they are high on the scale such as a newborn infant found alive in the rubble of a terrible earthquake that claimed thousands of lives and yet this tiny, fragile baby survived against all odds. Blessings tend to be much smaller than miracles, such as special people like a neighbor who brings you hot soup on a blustering cold day when you are feeling under the weather; or a special friend who accepts you as you are, and is unequivocally there anytime you need them. The beauty of a sunset or a splendidly colored rainbow after a dark and dreary storm is just a few of life's blessings or even miracles perhaps. Blessings come from many sources in our lives. We have to open our hearts to them and appreciate them no matter where we are emotionally at the time.

One thing I am sure of is the world today needs miracles and blessings more than ever, but especially those in our world who are struggling to live life with hope when darkness surrounds them. I am a part of an organization, Parents Of Murdered Children, dedicated to the ongoing emotional support of assisting parents, other family members and friends who have lost a child or loved one to murder. There is no one who needs more blessings and flat out miracles in their lives than those who have had their world shattered into pieces by someone who chose to take their loved ones violently from them. Then, there are also many people struggling with other difficult challenges of all kinds who need miracles and blessings too.

I have come to appreciate both the simplest blessings and greatest miracles in a whole new light since the murder of my own son, Brian. He was eighteen when he was robbed and shot to death while walking his girlfriend home in our neighborhood. While I was blessed with many children in my life and through my home day care, I still did not believe I could survive the pain of his loss. It is the most devastatingly, horrific event a parent can ever endure. Those children, however, allowed me to see the beauty and wonder in life, experiencing it through their innocence and trust, during a time when I felt my whole world shattered and the ground beneath me wavering on collapsing. I was always blessed with them in my life but never more so than at that particular time. I would, however, need many more blessings during the coming months and years ahead as I learned to live again after I was frozen in traumatic grief. I had to learn to recreate myself and rebuild my shattered world while grasping the hope that my family could remain intact, though I knew not how.

One of the many blessings, although I personally like to call them "journey gentlers," in those early times without my son came in the form of animals. My husband was outside on our horse property one day using his table saw to build something, though I don't remember exactly what. While sawing away a white dove fluttered down from its perch in the towering pine tree above my husband and landed gently on his shoulder. Shocked by such a strange event, my husband simply remained still, afraid the dove would fly away if he moved and not wanting to ruin this special moment. He also could not believe the noise of the saw did not frighten the dove off. Eventually, the dove did fly off my husband's shoulder but remained nearby walking on the ground near him as he continued to work; the noise of the power saw not bothering it at all. I came outside to check on my husband and got to experience this with him, capturing the moment as a special blessing, or again, "journey gentler," in our sorrow-filled hearts.

After that episode and for some time, whenever either my husband or I would go outside the dove would come to us where ever we were, either the front or back of our three-acre ranch property, and even on the front porch each morning when I brought the newspaper inside at the crack of dawn. It was as if it was sitting in the trees each

44

day waiting for us to come out. Every time my day care kids were playing inside, the dove would come to the front door window ledge, perch and watch the kids. It would sometimes peck at the window as if to get their attention and say hello. It was a beautiful and tender blessing and something we will never forget.

Not long after our son was killed but before the dove episode, a fluffy, snow-white bunny came up to my husband out of nowhere while he was working on our son's Mustang that he and Brian had been rebuilding. Unfortunately, they never got to finish it before our son was killed and this deeply bothered my husband. It took Don many months to pick up working on it again after Brian died as it was a tremendously difficult emotional task and a harsh reminder that he could no longer share it with his son. While working on the car this particular day though, the rabbit hopped right up to him at the car and he felt such comfort from it being there. It was as if his son was saying, "It will be okay, Dad." I believe that both animals were sent to comfort a grieving family, but especially my husband in his most dire time of need. Was it a blessing or a small miracle? Maybe that depends on how much it was needed at the time.

The most special blessing and miracle I received during the time of rebuilding my life after my son's death happened nearly five years later. I was in a hospital room, attending the birth of a baby who, as she was born, was placed directly into my awaiting arms. I was equally smiling and trembling as I embraced my newly born daughter through a special God-sent adoption. I felt such incredible and absolute joy at that moment. As the tears of joy poured down my face, I realized that five years before I truly believed joy was something I would never feel again. Yet, here I was reveling in it during this miracle of birth. It was such a pleasant surprise to know that I could experience joy again. It was repeated twice in the next few years with the eventual births of my two grandsons. Again my experience of absolute joy somehow made even more joyful because of the pain I had endured and a newly learned set of priorities in life. Life is about moments that take your breath away and bring healing to a broken heart and hope to a wounded, struggling soul.

Through the miracle of these births, I was reminded of the very first and greatest miracle of all time; the birth of a baby in a manger, a baby sent to save the world. Jesus' birth was the beginning of all miracles on this troubled earth and his birth brought forth the ultimate hope for all mankind from then on.

Did any of the blessings or miracles experienced by my family take away the pain of our son's loss? Of course not, but they reminded us that the beauty of hope exists all around us and most especially through the gifts received with each blessing. Each "journey gentler," blessing or miracle we were lucky enough to encounter helped slowly heal our broken hearts and remind us we could go on. While our hearts will never be fully healed we will always be grateful for each and every one of them that graced our life when we most desperately needed them.

"It is during our darkest moments that we must focus to see the light."
~ Aristotle Onassis

THUMBS UP
By Kim Chatfield

"The Golden Rule"

"Mommy," that is what my mother always was to me. She was kind, loving and positive to everyone around her and I don't remember her ever saying a judgmental thing about anyone. To me she was the best mom. She was a homemaker to her three daughters with me being her "baby."

My mother Ann was born Jewish and proud of her heritage, but she was not religious. Most of her friends were also Jewish but that was a matter of geography. My mother raised us with "The Golden Rule": treat others as you would like to be treated. She loved us and was always there for us no matter what. She and my father had a loving marriage and I remember a lot of laughter between them.

On a very special day, my mother and I happened to be watching *King of Kings* in her bedroom. I was a teenager and she was in her forties. I remember that we both cried during the crucifixion and I turned to her and said that I believed in Christ and what they said he did for us. She acknowledged this as well. This was most unusual especially since no one ever talked to us about Christ. Although we were born Jewish, we just believed and had faith in Christ on that day.

When my father died at a young age, my mother moved to an active condominium development in Florida. She learned quickly how to do so many things that my father had done in their marriage and the inner strength she always had manifested itself in her day-to-day living. She was always active and health conscious, and played tennis, golf and walked. She made friends quickly and was happy. While she dated a bit, she never had another romantic relationship. This did not bother her at all.

It was in her 50's that she started on her spiritual growth and it grew in Florida. She read the Bible, watched her favorite inspirational TV ministers, and grew as a child of God. She never realized how this spiritual nourishment was going to get her through the darkest part of her life and ours as well.

"Don't Stop Believing"

At age 70 and with what seemed to come out of nowhere, my mother was stricken with ALS. It is a progressive neurodegenerative disease that affects nerve cells in the brain and spinal cord. It kills you by killing your motor neurons and muscle function. There is no cure. My mother started to have deterioration in her speech.

So many of the things we do and take for granted such as talking and eating become impossible. The heartbreak to watch someone you love deteriorate in such a horrible way truly can't be put into words.

While I am sure that my mother had her private moments of intense sadness, she remained positive and never stopped loving God or believing in a miracle. She continued to feed her mind and heart with God's word throughout all of it.

Since there is no cure for this disease, we three sisters ended up taking my mother to Mexico for alternative treatments. Sadly, it did not help. My sister Dale was now living in the same development as my mother so she became her caregiver. Dale was the oldest and had a special friendship with my mother.

We saw our mother continue to deteriorate. Her speech was affected by the disease and she eventually had to write things down to communicate. We could no longer pick up the phone and call her to say hello and have her say hello back.

My mother had a signal for us that she would do to let us know that she was doing ok. It was making a "Thumbs Up" sign (two thumbs pointing up to heaven).

Can you imagine wanting to have a simple conversation with someone and physically not being able to? Can you imagine the words not coming out and the frustration and helplessness it would cause? And what about eating? It's another thing that we do and enjoy every day without giving it a thought. Can you imagine not physically being able to eat, or chew or swallow? About a year into her disease, my mother had to have a feeding tube inserted into her body.

Shortly before her death, about a year and a half after of the disease's onset, my mother was at home and couldn't breathe. She was rushed to the hospital where a tracheotomy had to be performed. I was living in New Jersey at the time and flew down when this happened. I will never forget walking into the rehabilitation center where they brought her after this procedure. My heart and spirit sank to the lowest point imaginable when I saw her hooked up to machines and the look on her face was one of sadness. I felt a helplessness that was overwhelming and I could not hold back the tears.

I remember sitting on the bed with my mother and telling her how much I loved her. I asked her if she wanted me to find a mercy killing doctor. I don't know if I would have followed through with it but at the time I believe I would have done anything to end her suffering. She wrote on her notepad "No, God will take care of it." Even through all of this, that was her belief and her heart. I remember praying on her bed with my sister Dale as well. We all held hands and thanked God for his love and I remember saying that no matter what happens we always love God. All of us shook our heads yes. That was how we felt in our hearts. Before we left my mother, we told her how much we loved her.

The following day before getting to the rehabilitation center, we received a call from them that our mother was rushed to the hospital. They could not tell us anything else, but we thought we would see her alive one more time. That was not going to happen.

When we got to the hospital we were told that she had died at the rehabilitation center, but the hospital had put her on life support. When we walked in and saw her hooked up to a breathing machine I lost it. I started screaming for them to take her off life support as she had a DNR form but we did not have it with us. I don't remember how we got the form but we did and they took her off the machine. My sister Dale stayed with my mother while the doctors stopped the machine. I could not bear to.

"Something Good From Something Bad"

That was a saying that I grew up hearing from my mom. The truth of those words came true to me and my sister Dale after my mother died of ALS.

The day after my mother's death, Dale and I went back to the rehabilitation facility to find the nurse who had seen my mother alive for the last time. Remember that the day before she died she was so very sad but believed that God would take care of her and that we always love God no matter what.

Dale and I found out that the nurse who last saw my mother alive was Sonia. We waited to speak to Sonia so we could ask her how my mother was the day she died. What she told us changed our lives forever. Sonia had never met my mother before and knew nothing about her or her illness.

When we sat down with Sonia we asked her how our mother was doing before she died. Sonia said, "When I saw your mother that morning she was happy, she was smiling and doing "this." It was then that Sonia made the "Thumbs Up" gesture to me and Dale.

49

Well, we cried tears of joy because we knew that only a miracle could have brought my mother from sadness to happiness. It was a miracle for us because God knew we couldn't bear to have our last image of her in the state that we saw her the day before. Not only that, we believe within the depths of our hearts that God, Jesus and the angels came to her at some point after we left and took her back to her spiritual home. Sonia also told us that she left my mother's room for only a couple of minutes that morning and when she came back my mother had passed away. We believe that someday she will get to tell us what happened and we know that it had to be an experience so beautiful that she would be happy, smiling and "Thumbs Up."

"At times our own light goes out and is rekindled by a spark from another person. Each of us has cause to think with deep gratitude of those who have lighted the flame within us." ~Albert Schweitzer

THE HEALER
By Liz Dolan

Four-year-old David who has Downs
snuggles into three-year-old

Tommy's chest like a Maine coon cat.
Then he pets Tommy's head

flubs his lips on his pale cheek
and laughs at the noise it makes

with so much heart, he warms ours.
Even though he knows Tommy

cannot move nor speak, unlike us
he does not give up hope for him

maybe recalling when he himself
sipped air raggedly through a trach

and could not pedal his trike
but how last night in falling twilight

he did.

MR. X & MR. Y
By Elynne Chaplik-Aleskow

It often happens like that. Strangers regularly meet in the same place by coincidence or necessity and share discourse on some level. It might be small talk or profound thoughts. It might be politics or current events. It might be shoptalk or gossip. The one constant is that the strangers do not exchange names.

So it was for these two men. Both were lawyers. Every few weeks they met in the hallway of the courthouse. They shared discussions of their upcoming cases. Both were defense attorneys. One was devoted to helping the underprivileged. He was a private attorney who would take a case whether his client could pay him or not. The other often helped his countrymen who like himself had come to the United States to make their home.

These two men were old-fashioned gentlemen. They were from the old school of manners and dedication. They loved the law and even more loved helping people. In time they related like old friends.

Mr. X was a Russian immigrant who came to the United States when he was in his teens. He put himself through college and law school and created his legal practice. Word spread throughout the community that he was a caring and empathic lawyer. He had a wife who was a concert pianist and a son who was the gift of his life. He and his wife called their son their dividend.

Mr. Y was married with two sons. He was born to practice law. He was a man who loved to talk and who believed in the essence of justice and fairness. He was exemplary in his legal work. He was a champion of the poor.

Mr. Y was attracted to Mr. X's style and demeanor. Mr. X wore pince-nez glasses. He was dignified with an old world charm and grace. Mr. Y loved their talks as they waited to appear in court. They had become two friendly strangers who knew nothing of one another but the fact that they were both attorneys.

Years later Mr. X died. Mr. Y looked for his friend but finally realized something must have happened to him.

One night Mr. Y who was my Uncle Sam Linn was invited to my fiancé's mother's home for dinner to celebrate our engagement. As my uncle walked into my future mother-in-law's dining room, he looked at a large oil portrait hanging on the wall. He stared at the painting almost unable to speak.

"Is this your husband?" he asked stunned.

My fiancé answered first.

"Yes, that is my father, Gregory Aleskow."

"I knew him from court," my uncle responded. "He was an elegant man. We used to talk all the time in the courthouse hallway. I liked him so very much."

We all stood looking at the portrait of my future husband Richard's father.

"I cannot believe this," my uncle said softly almost speaking to himself.

"I knew him and loved talking to him."

We celebrated two occasions that night. We made a special toast to the reunion of two friends who shared a mutual admiration and through fate were about to become relatives through marriage.

Previously published in *Forever Friends* (Mandinam Press)

"Gratitude is the healthiest of all human emotions. The more you express gratitude for what you have, the more likely you will have even more to express gratitude for." ~ Zig Ziglar

LIGHT-BRINGER/TORCH-BEARER

By Juley Harvey

mom
always brought the light,
the candles,
the hurricane lantern, the tablecloth,
the gilded lilies
to the table,
to the room,
filled the wherever.
the torch winkingly passes;
it is not enough to allay the gloom.
but it is
something of a mouse,
as she said,
breathed
into the house.
and so it goes,
not quite flows
(perhaps ice floes),
but light
will not be dead.
it shimmers,
dances
in heart and head,
all around,
denying the drab dank dark.
light is a lark,
a lamb you cannot slaughter
or douse;

it is too subtle
in its insistence,
too stubborn,
and knows from whence
it came.
too containable,
too uncontained,
just like mom,
too big
a heart
for this world.
so on to the next,
all-seeing, knowing,
being, fixing, baking,
making it all right,
at the speed
of angel light,
with the momentous mom might.
somewhere
she's in bright flight.
good night,
sweet princess hat.

MARRIED TO A NURSE
By William S. Creed

How lucky I am? Not only does my bride love me to death, she's a nurse! If I get sick, she will lovingly nurse me back to health; you know, bring me warm drinks, tuck the covers under my chin, and kiss my fevered brow. She'll probably peek in the door and say, "Anything I can get you, honey?" How lucky can a guy get?

Every time I get a sniffle, out comes the blood pressure cuff and stethoscope. She actually keeps them at home! "It may not be a simple cold, it may be pneumonia," she says. But, it goes on beyond that. A sore back may be Radiculopathy (what the hell is that?). If I have trouble remembering, could be Senescent Changes or Cerebellar Atrophy. Shrinking brains for heaven sake!

A simple headache could be Cephalgia, Cerebella Edema, or Hematoma which could lead to a stroke! My God woman, stop speaking in five-syllable words and just bring me a little something warm to drink and kiss my brow!

It reached its peak one day when I was scheduled to be in a charity golf tournament at the local golf course. I made the mistake of complaining that I had a little chest pain which might affect with my golf swing – you know the common gas pains one has from time to time. I hoped she had some antacid I could take. The average person would understand that – not my wife, the nurse.

Out came those dreaded instruments again, followed by, "You need to get to the hospital and get checked out."

"It's gas, woman, simple gas!"

Did she think I was going to give up a golf game to get my gas measured? We had a rather intense conversation in which I agreed to give up the golf game, my sense of independence, my manhood, and every other damn thing and go the hospital. A man needs some peace!

At the hospital the doctor and I shared sympathies regarding wives. He then performed an emergency six-vessel bypass. Later, he told me if I'd gone golfing, I would not have made it off the golf course alive.

Turns out, my wife not only loves me to death, she loves me to life.

MY BATTLE CRY
By Vanessa A. Jackson Austin

As I fall on my knees,
Father God, I pray,
Help me fight this cancerous disease.

For I need you in a mighty, mighty way
As I journey through this life
Each and every day.

Because I know nothing about the road ahead
But with my eyes focused on you,
I am spirit led.

For I know with you as my protector
And my guide
Without a doubt, I will survive.

Because as I continue to trust in you
My Faith will help me
Make the journey through.

For you promised never to leave me
Nor forsake me,
So I must always remember that trusting you
Is the key.

Previously published in *Cries in the Wind* (WestBow Press)

MIRACLE ON A COUNTRY ROAD
By TK Alvarez

To this day, nineteen years later, I can clearly see that railroad crossing on a country road in Indiana. I see myself driving my aunt's car across that track with no thought that a train was careening toward the intersection I was about to cross. I can still feel the gut-wrenching terror as I watched helplessly in the rear-view mirror. My sixteen-year-old daughter was following close behind with her brother and two cousins.

The kids and I had come to Indiana from Illinois for a week-long vacation to visit family at my cousin's lake cottage. First we stopped to pick up my favorite aunt. As it turned out, my cousin's two sons were visiting her (their grandmother) and so would be traveling back to their lake cottage with us. We decided we would need to drive two cars since there were six of us plus all the paraphernalia we would be hauling along.

I had a cute little four seat red convertible which my family loved to call my mid-life car. After some deliberation about who would ride with whom, we decided that I would drive my aunt's vehicle and she would co-pilot us up to the cottage. We would allow all three boys to ride with my daughter, Cassie, in the convertible. After all, they would be following us and would always be in sight. Cassie had proven to be a very conscientious youthful driver and the day was clear and sunny, so it seemed like a fun solution for all of us. Besides, I was eager to catch up on all the family happenings with my aunt. This way she and I would have two hours of uninterrupted conversation. Later I would realize all that talking had distracted me from being as alert and watchful as I should have been on a country road that was not the least familiar.

In Illinois, railroad crossings have lights or crossing arms at intersections. As I would learn later, this was not always the case in Indiana, at least not at that time. In that state, it was the vehicle operator's responsibility to stop at those crossings and look for approaching trains.

I remember noticing a house to my left as I approached that fateful crossing and a thick grove of pine trees lining the track up to the road on which I was traveling. I think now that grove of trees was probably planted many years before to shield the view of those tracks from that house. Unfortunately, they shielded the view of drivers too. As I crossed that track, without slowing down a whit, I saw the train bearing down on that intersection at an alarming speed. As soon as I crossed, I screamed, "Oh Dear God!" It was all I had time to get out. However, my mind was racing. I realized in that instant that my daughter would not stop either. She would follow her mother's lead – and she did. There was just no way those kids would make it and I knew it deep in my soul.

As I watched in my rear view mirror, horrified, that little red car made it across! I could see that giant train whoosh past right behind my precious children and their cousins; all the while blasting its ominous warning horn. By the time I managed to stop the car and run back to see how they were, I was weeping and trembling. My darling girl was sure she was in trouble but it was all *my* fault! In an instant, we came terribly close to losing all four of those children. To speak of it even now can cause tears of shame.

It was my ten-year-old son, Jeff, who told me that as they crossed the track, everything became as if in slow motion. He saw the train right next to his window but it seemed to be stopped. Then an instant later they were across and the train was speeding away behind them. None of us has forgotten that incident all those years ago. We know that God in His mercy and mystery and love spared those children that day. And whenever I recall those terrifying moments, I am at once filled with awe and joy and love for a holy God who heard my desperate cry.

MIRACLE
By Lynn C. Johnston

If you had asked me in 2006 what road my life would take, I never could have anticipated most of the events that occurred. That year, my always healthy mother was diagnosed with pancreatic cancer and succumbed to the disease seven months later. I was laid off from my job six weeks after the funeral. The next few years didn't get any better with only temporary job prospects and deepening financial woes.

I thought I had pretty much hit rock bottom. Then in the fall of 2009, my precious indoor Calico cat, Valentine, got outside and vanished.

Feeling like my nightmare was only getting worse, I was tormented with visions of all the horrible things she could encounter. Had she been injured by another animal or a car? Was she being held against her will? Was she getting enough food?

I plastered the neighborhood with flyers and knocked on nearly every door, meeting most of my neighbors for the first time. As I showed them her picture, their faces fell, often recalling their own agony of a lost pet. I asked that if they were religiously inclined to please keep Valentine's safe return in their prayers.

My teenage son and I roamed the neighborhood every night with flashlights, just hoping to catch a glimpse of her. And each night when we returned home unsuccessful, I was heartbroken. As the days dragged on, my hopes and faith were fading. I was crushed. It seemed as if God was kicking me when I was down.

But one night, three weeks to the day after she disappeared, my son announced that he heard her collar bell ringing outside. My heart leapt.

"Are you sure?" I said, too afraid to have my hopes dashed again.

"Yes, and I saw her. It was dark, but I'm sure it was her." He went on to say that she ran into the yard of the apartment building next door.

When he said that, I spontaneously broke into tears. I couldn't stop crying. She wasn't home yet, but at least I knew she was alive and healthy enough to run.

The next day we rented a humane animal trap from our local shelter and set it outside that night. I filled it with small chucks of Kentucky Fried Chicken (as they recommended), and placed an old baby monitor next to the trap in hopes I would hear it snap closed. Then I prayed for a miracle. Too anxious to even sleep in my own bed, I slept on the living room sofa so I could be near our front door.

At three o'clock in the morning, my prayers were answered. Valentine was in the trap, filthy, scared, and about three pounds lighter than she left us. I was never so happy to see her in my life.

I dropped to my knees and thanked God for bringing her home safely and bringing her light back into my life. It was a miracle.

Five years later, Valentine is still with us, happy and healthy. There is not a day that goes by that I do not remember those three harrowing weeks and thank God for her return,

Valentine and God taught me two valuable lessons that have helped sustain me in times of crisis ever since: Miracles do happen and nightmares can have happy endings.

Previously published in *Nurturing Paws* (Whispering Angel Books)

"What you focus on expands, and when you focus on the goodness in your life, you create more of it. Opportunities, relationships, even money flowed my way when I learned to be grateful no matter what happened in my life."
~ *Oprah Winfrey*

INTENSIVE CARE
By Louise Webster

Never had I been so sick
A head that I could barely lift
Legs so shaky and so weak
I could not walk, just barely creep

The hospital took me right away
But it was doubtful if I'd stay
Breathing was so very hard
Every beat wore at my heart

The doctors merely shook their heads
Sure that by morning I'd be dead
I felt myself loosed from the pain
As I rose to another plain

Brightness soon surrounded me
All was peaceful as could be
I felt the prayers of loved ones dear
Though gravely ill, I knew no fear

Somehow this was not my time
Without doubt I would survive
In miracles I do believe
And angels who watch over me

THE ANGEL'S SILENT PROMISE
By Sharon S. Fulham

"For He will give His angels charge over you to accompany
and defend and preserve you in all of your ways." ~ Psalm 91:11

I have always been fascinated by the inspiring painting of "The Guardian Angel," protecting two children crossing a dangerous bridge, attributed to Lindberg. This comforting painting portrays a "silent promise" that angels watch over children in dangerous situations. I believe that my Guardian Angel protected me at the young age of eight when I wandered away from a family picnic, and nearly drowned in the Eel River. It was a sunny Memorial Day weekend in the early fifties.

Giant redwood trees lined both sides of curvy 'old highway 101' en route to Richardson's Grove Park. Throughout the park, majestic redwood trees kept us spellbound. Stately oak and flourishing pine trees were scattered everywhere. Evergreen Bay trees looked like flourishing shrubbery. Purple wildflowers and tropical ivy made me feel like I was in a spacious magical garden. We were 75 miles away from home and we were excited!!!

My sister, brother and I were close in age, and very playful and rambunctious. We headed straight for the river soon after our arrival. My youngest sister remained with my parents in the shade near the river. We played hard and long in the warm sun, snacked on the run, and slurped cold water. We splashed and waded close to the riverbank, then later ventured further out, up to our knees. The river flowed gently and was clear enough for us to see "rock treasures" at the bottom. We splashed each other and tossed pebbles high and far across the river to see who could throw the farthest. My brother always won!

For no logical reason other than the desire to explore, I began wading in cool water up to my knees toward a patch of bushy bay trees at the bank of the river. The feel of the squishy sand and smooth rocks against my bare feet felt soothing. The river ripples brushed against by lower legs tickling them as I happily explored.

Gradually the river reached my waist. I was having the time of my life and therefore, not concerned. The river had taken a slight curve and clusters of Bay trees at the river bank blocked my siblings from view. I had not realized I had ventured out too far. Thankfully, I could still hear a faint chorus of voices. I decided to go back even though I felt safe. Wrong! When I turned I stepped into a sandy downward slope which caused the water to quickly rise to my chest. I could not swim and I became petrified! My heart pounded! I was afraid to scream for fear of losing my balance and sinking deeper. No one even knew I was nearly under water.

Panic stricken and shivering I looked all around wondering what to do. At the brink of toppling over, I noticed something incredible! Swaying in the cool breeze was a sunlit overgrown branch with leafy limbs which appeared out of nowhere. It extended toward me as if inviting me to grab hold and hang on. I quickly reached for it clutching tightly with both hands. With adrenalin pumping I pulled and pulled until I was out of the deepest part of the water. Miraculously, the sturdy flexible branch had become my lifeline and prevented me from drowning. I clearly remember feeling relieved, exhilarated, anxious and weary all at the same time! Very carefully I trekked in shallow water toward my siblings, all of whom were still romping in cool water. I surmised that I had not been "out of sight" long enough for anyone to miss me. Even so, I was grateful to be alive!!!

I had not shared my story with anyone, until recently. I kept it locked away as a private experience of utter helplessness, and of feeling alone in chest-deep water. On the other hand, the realization that God sent His angel to rescue me through an unforeseen overgrown branch is extremely comforting, and exhilarating! His caring protection on my behalf still moves me to this day.

It's a sobering thought that parents cannot always be close-by when children face life threatening circumstances. This is why I am so touched by the painting of "The Guardian Angel" protecting two children on a dangerous bridge. It beautifully portrays the "silent promise" that God sends His angels to watch over children in grave danger. Every time I see the famous painting, I remember how I almost drowned and that my guardian angel was there protecting me.

There are some people who see angels and others who do not. In my own situation, I saw the "evidence" that my guardian angel had been there through an "unexpected" overgrown branch which became my lifeline. To this day, the painting comforts me with its "silent promise" that God's intervention is real! He sends His angels to watch over children in dangerous situations. I know because I was one of those helpless children at the young age of eight years old.

A FIGHTING SPIRIT

By William Lacewell, Jr.

You are a light to get us through the darkness.
You are the beacon to get us through the storm.
You reinforce our strength in times of trouble.
You guide us through Gods' plan, for us to reform.

My life had been filled with obstacles,
Sometimes I didn't know which way to turn.
You helped me find the right path in life.
You let me know that I still have a lot to learn.

I appreciate your teachings and friendship,
You've helped me more than you'll ever know.
I know that I have to put my trust in God,
He wants us to be humble in order to grow.

Thank you and your family for being in my life,
You've helped me gain strength that I needed.
I may still stumble or fall from time to time,
But I won't be down for the count, and defeated.

I HOPE YOU DANCE

By Carolyn T. Johnson

Based on LeeAnn Womack's "I Hope You Dance"

Looking up at the stage from our fifth row floor seats was unbelievable. George Strait and Reba McEntire were going to rock the world tonight. The air was palpable. Julianna Hough and Blake Shelton were slated as warm-up entertainers but the King and Queen of Country took top billing. I was so excited, I could hardly contain myself.

The announcer came on the stage welcoming everyone, then said, "Unfortunately Julianna Hough has laryngitis and will not be performing tonight so to kick off this great event, please help me welcome a very special, last minute guest, Ms. Lee Ann Womack."

I couldn't believe my ears. My eyes deceived me. There she stood, in the flesh, Lee Ann Womack. She wowed the crowd with her familiar upbeat tunes then the lights dimmed for her slow song. I knew which one she was going to sing. I knew every word by heart. It was personal. That song was me.

I hope you never lose your sense of wonder. At the allergist's office, I always stop to smell the roses growing in the little triangle surrounded by miles of cement. Amazed at how emaciated they look to smell so sweet.

I hope you get your fill to eat but never lose that hunger. After a successful banking career, I dove into the deep end of creative writing. I longed to express myself in the written word, to make the reader get to the last line and want more.

May you never take one single breath for granted. I wake each morning to kiss my husband goodbye before he leaves for the office, just in case it's the last kiss from those lips.

God forbid love ever leaves you empty handed. I've learned from my past loves and taken the best of each lesson going forward.

I hope you still feel small when you stand by the ocean. I've mentored two young students, who needed a friend to talk to, in hopes of making a difference in this world, one child at a time.

When one door closes, I hope one more opens. I believe, in my heart, that opportunity still exists, even in defeat. That's why a loved one's suicide still haunts me.

Promise me you'll give fate a fighting chance. Hard work and preparation are worthy endeavors, but fate's the critical component in the equation. The combination has brought me success in my career, a fulfilling marriage and an abundant life.

I hope you never fear those mountains in the distance. I've procrastinated, but I've never been afraid to fail. I've submitted my essays and poems to noteworthy publications because all they could do was say no. I've taken my satisfaction in trying.

Never settle for the path of least resistance. I've left friends to attend college out of state, lived overseas as a nineteen-year-old exchange student, and even moved to a city, where I had only one friend, to resurrect my banking career. The moves weren't easy, but provided adventurous new beginnings.

Living might mean taking chances but they're worth taking. I've ridden a Harley Davidson at seventy-five miles-an-hour through the Hill Country of Texas with a smile plastered on my face.

Loving might be a mistake but it's worth making. I've loved deeply, failed miserably, and found the love I needed all along.

Don't let some hell bent heart leave you bitter. I've watched friends harbor such hatred and distrust of men that they miss out one of the best parts of life.

When you come close to selling out, reconsider. I've put one foot in front of the other, following a disastrous marriage, a miserable job, and the death of my father. I've carefully reconstructed the broken pieces of my life to become whole again.

Give the heavens above more than just a passing glance. I have faith in an abundant God, a loving God, a forgiving God.

*And when you get a chance to sit it out or dance, I hope you dance....*The final note rang in my ears. Tears streamed down my face. I was breathless. At a loss for words. Grateful to be understood so completely. Delighted to dance.

SOMETHING HOLY

By Cherise Wyneken

Two hour surgery, lasted six.
Two night stay – two months.
Complications snowballed
like dust mites without a ray of sun.
Multi-system organ failure.
No chance with surgery, but they'll try.

Terror snatched me from my robin's nest,
grabbed my throat with its beak, and squeezed
my breath away like water from a sponge.
Prayers flew up from many faiths
to the god they knew. Doubt crept in behind
and seesawed in my echo chamber.

Next week – same scene.
No time to stop the gurney, grinding toward OR,
for me to give a good-bye kiss.
Tubes in his side for nourishment,
tubes in his throat for air,
tubes to his veins recycling blood.
> *We are together in this room –*
> *a walled-in box, filled with monitors*
> *and IV bags dripping blue solution.*
> *We are together in this room,*
> *yet we are far apart.*
> *I cannot see inside your head.*
> *I cannot hear your thoughts.*
> *Your voice is trapped within.*
> *I am here beside you – alone.*
May crept into June.
July brought plans for a nursing home

readied with a respirator – possibly for life.
Certain he could manage without machines,
refusing to give up, Nurse Debby
disconnects the oxygen, watches as he breathes.
Three weeks later, unplugged, learning to use his legs,
able to swallow soup and applesauce,
I brought the car around for a man alive.

SUNNY SIDE UP
By Paul Cummins
for Avani Rose Colella Cummins, born August 3, 2012

"Sunny side up," the pediatrician
proclaimed, pulling back the curtain
of your mother's belly, and there,

there you were, staring up,
making your debut upon the stage
of this magical, fractured world,

staring into the bright lights.
May you stay sunny side up,
night or day, whatever the play.

LESSON IN THE SNOW
By Deborah LeFalle

The year was 1974 and I was heading back to college after winter break. I had traveled home to California by airplane for the Christmas holidays with plans to drive my car back to Wisconsin where I was attending graduate school. With my boyfriend accompanying me, we set out from San Jose on a Wednesday morning in my 1972 Volkswagen bug packed to capacity. We figured the road trip would take us about four days to reach Milwaukee, and we had mapped out stopping points where we would gas up, restaurants where we would dine, and motels where we would lodge along the way. We brought along water and other beverages to keep us hydrated, and plenty of healthy snacks to ward off any potential hunger pangs. We were dressed warmly, and I had made sure the car was in tip-top shape so we wouldn't encounter any mechanical problems. I had even bought four new snow tires. Not accustomed to being in a cold climate, however, there was one important precaution I did not take. We would find out what this was on our third night into the trip.

So here we are driving at night on Interstate 80 east through Iowa toward our stop for the night in Des Moines. It is snowing and the temperature is hovering at some unimaginable number of degrees below zero. Oblivious to our impending plight, we are cruising along when the car unexpectedly starts to putt, stall and backfire. The engine gradually loses power and despite repeated efforts to accelerate, our speed decreases to a crawl. We veer toward the road shoulder and the car eventually comes to a complete stop. We try several times to restart the engine, but it simply will not turn over. It will not budge. We think it is dead. We look at each other in a quandary as if to say, "Now what?" The sky is dark and electric lights are few. By now the snow is falling more heavily and we surmise we are in the beginnings of a snowstorm. As treacherous as the weather is, my boyfriend steps out of the car and ankle-deep in snow, walks around to the back engine hatch. He opens the hatch and peers inside looking for anything out of the ordinary.

Finding nothing amiss, he quickly retreats back inside the car to get out of the frigid cold. This is when we decide our best bet is to sit tight until help arrives.

With the temperature inside the car dropping rapidly, our first concern is to stay warm. Though bundled up in our winter coats, gloves, boots, and caps, we are still extremely cold. We are shivering. Feeling as if frostbite is overtaking our appendages, we remove our boots, turn our bodies sideways so we're face-to-face, and we wedge our feet under each other's butt. We cross our arms over our chests and slide our hands under our respective armpits. Our logic is that our naturally generated body heat might bring us some level of relief. We both become very quiet. It is after midnight and Friday has now become Saturday. The highway is desolate. I wonder... Will my car be covered in snow and nobody be able to find us? Will our toes and fingers freeze to a point of having to amputate them? Will we be stranded here, left alone the entire night?

God must have been smiling down on us because in less than an hour a highway patrol officer spots us and pulls his vehicle up behind ours. We cannot be happier – we are saved! We explain to the officer what happened and provide him with our driver's licenses, registration, and insurance information. Sensing our distress, he offers us a blanket and calmly reassures us we will be safe and warm soon. He sees my tears and reaches into his coat pocket to produce an unopened mini-pack of facial tissues. Seconds later, he radios in to have a tow truck dispatched, and asks the dispatcher to alert the owners of the nearest motel that we will need accommodations for the night. The highway patrol officer leaves once the tow truck driver is on site and has been briefed, but not before we thank him profusely for his assistance.

We ride with the tow truck driver to the next town – about a fifteen-minute drive – talking about the snowstorm practically the entire way. A huge neon VACANCY sign comes into view as we approach the tiny motel. The establishment looks to be a typical mom and pop business, and our hunch is soon confirmed when we walk inside to find the owners waiting up for us with hot tea they have prepared. We tip the driver, and he continues on to the local auto repair shop where my car will be worked on the following day. Ready for a good night's sleep, we bid the owners goodnight and retreat to our cozy room without further ado.

We rise mid-morning to the smell of hot coffee and freshly baked banana bread. Through the motel room window we see that the storm has eased to where only a few snowflakes are gently falling. We groom and dress ourselves quickly, pack our belongings, and then join the motel owners in the compact lobby. We help ourselves to the coffee and banana bread they have made, and sit and chat for a few minutes before setting out on foot toward the auto repair shop a quarter-mile up the road.

Upon our 11:00 AM arrival at the shop, the time we agreed to meet up, we curiously observe the Hours of Operation sign in the shop's window indicates they are closed on weekends. Nonetheless, we walk right in. To our surprise we find that the mechanic on duty is the tow truck driver from night before! "The car is ready," he proclaims with a wide grin. I ask about the shop hours, and standing very proudly he replies in a majestic-sounding voice, "I came in today Ma'am, to work on your car and your car alone." A wave of gratitude flushes over me. Undeniably, I am glad he made this sage choice. Diagnosis: frozen gas line, requiring the line to be flushed and the oil changed to a lighter weight. We pay for the repair and express our sincere appreciation to the mechanic/tow truck driver for going beyond the call of duty for us. Before hitting the highway we make one last stop back at the motel to retrieve our luggage, settle our lodging bill, and thank the elderly couple for their hospitality. They thank us in return for our patronage, wish us well on continuing our journey, and give us a baggie full of chocolate candy kisses for the road.

The lesson we learned from this experience is more than the obvious of being schooled on how oil weight can affect an automobile's road performance in extreme climate conditions. The greater lesson is a reminder of how good-natured people can be. The everyday people we encountered – the highway patrol officer, the tow truck driver/mechanic, and the motel owners – were simply doing their jobs. Yes, they were doing their jobs, but moreover, they were doing them admirably. Their humble gestures of empathy and understanding toward us two naïve travelers from sunny California did not go unnoticed. My boyfriend and I were very much aware that our ordeal could have turned out much worse than it did, and that we were fortunate to have eluded danger essentially unscathed. We were, and I still am, very grateful for the considerate people who selflessly came to our aid at that juncture in our lives... a true testament to the divine and intrinsic goodness in humankind.

GOD'S GRACE
By Vanessa A. Jackson Austin

Nothing but Grace kept me,
During my time of sickness and recovery.

Nothing but Grace held me close,
God's Amazing Grace wouldn't let me go.

Nothing but Grace kept me here,
Because His Amazing Grace is always near.

Nothing but Grace held my hand,
God's Amazing Grace gave me another chance.

Nothing but Grace kept me sane,
As I know my suffering was not in vain.

God's Amazing Grace will never fail,
Because His Love and Grace will "always" prevail.

CHURCH IN THE DALE
By Harry P. Noble, Jr.

Clyde's headlights swung up our family lane. At three in the morning I should have been asleep, but I was up and charged with excitement. I met him at the front gate. Throwing my fishing gear in the back of his jeep, I said, "I'm ready!"

There was four years difference in our ages – he was twenty-two and I was eighteen. He was four years older, a recent veteran of World War II, including Omaha Beach on D-day. I was a bit in awe, and completely surprised when he asked me to go fishing, but had no trouble saying, "Yes."

The half-moon was shining but the night was still black. The jeep's headlights were powerful, and labored with passion, but unable to carve a tunnel of visibility more than a hundred feet ahead. The dash light was out so we couldn't see the speedometer, but Clyde said we were going thirty miles per hour.

Upon arrival, and looking to the east, I could see a weak smear of predawn. Following the narrow beam of a three-C-cell flashlight, we began making our way along the banks of an abandoned riverbed. Early light rays enabled us to see the magnificent trees that grew to the west. The trees, festooned with beards of gray moss, watched the sun as it labored at its daily chore of climbing the sky.

As additional morning light leached in, I was surprised to see a squadron of water striders skittering about over the water's surface. Also known as pond skaters, water scooters, skimmers, or Jesus bugs, they distinguish themselves by displaying the ability to walk on water.

A fog tried to sneak in, tiptoeing among the trees while cloaked in an immense stillness. The morning sun brought with it a gentle breeze that found the open throat of my shirt and spun out a warm caress, while chasing the fog away.

By 10:30 we had caught our limits and began loading our equipment for the journey home. Towering virgin hardwoods formed a scene of Mother Nature unmolested by the avarice of mankind. Her beauty spoke to us through silence; and we rode in that quiet, knowing nothing we could say would be an improvement.

As we emerged from the river bottom log-truck ruts on to a dirt road, our eyes locked on the unbelievable. To our left, on a slight rise, framed among giant white oaks and hickory-nut trees, stood "the little brown church in the vale," except it was white. It was an overwhelming surprise to come upon a square, one room frame building with four wooden windows and two doors in those deep piney woods. But the stunning feature, producing a surge of amazement that prompted Clyde to whip off the road, park under a massive sweet gum, and both of us stare, was the al fresco scene that turned the time-clock back two generations.

Tied to a hitching post in front of the little church were seven two-mule teams harnessed to wagons and six saddled horses; but not a single gasoline powered vehicle of any kind. Neither Clyde nor I uttered a word, too engrossed in our serendipitous look back into the nineteenth century.

As we sat there with our eyes flipping through pages of past generations we suddenly realized our ears were being offered an even greater epiphany. Those inside, with all four windows and both doors open, were singing "The Gospel Train" a cappella, embellished with 'shouts,' hand clapping and foot tapping. Switching our senses from visual to audio, we sat, transfixed. Out of that little church in the Wildwood came the highest quality spiritual singing either of us had ever heard.

As "The Gospel Train" ended, our ears were exposed to an even more profound treat as a deep male voice called a verse of "Swing Low Sweet Chariot" and the congregation answered with another verse. After several exchanges the singers slid into a 'swing' rhythm with "I'm Troubled in Mind." Just when we thought their magic had been expended and was at an end, the congregation elevated to even a higher level as they sang, "His Eye is on the Sparrow."

When that masterpiece came to a close and our breathing returned to an acceptable pace, Clyde started the jeep and we resumed our journey. Transported by those visual and auditory masterstrokes, for the next twenty miles we communicated entirely with dead silence. We didn't need words for what we had just seen or heard. Our memories were so deeply etched they sang a cappella together.

THE INFALLIBLE BRIDGE
By Janice Canerdy

I once was lost and floundering.
I couldn't find my way.
The One who walked upon the sea
became my Bridge, my stay.

God's Spirit spoke straight to my heart.
I asked Him to come in.
He plucked me from the troubled sea
engulfing me--my sin.

The only Bridge to God is He
who died upon the cross.
The unique love of Christ alone
can wash away the dross.

Some strongholds are reliable,
but there is only One
that proves to be infallible.
That Bridge is God's own Son.

COVERING THE BASES
By Jim Pahz

Let me say at the outset that my father is not Catholic, despite his propensity for medals, relics, and rosary beads. Actually, my dad is not much of anything at all when it comes to religion. If you asked him what faith he practiced he would think long and hard. There wouldn't be an automatic response. Then, he would say something like secular humanist – which is to say he believes in everything and nothing. He doesn't rely on supernatural forces or religious dogma. He likes to go his own way and is big on the scientific method.

So now that I've established what my father is not, I can tell you what he is. He is a collector. His mind doesn't dwell on theosophical matters, but on the here and now, and the things he can hold in his hands. And he has a lot in his hands and even more stuff in his desk drawer. My dad collects all kinds of things. He buys many of them from eBay. Each week little packages arrive in the mail. In the last few weeks he has collected badges (law enforcement and firemen's badges), brass plaques, necklaces from India, and most recently, religious medals. But Dad doesn't buy individual items; he buys stuff in lots. His last purchase consisted of 85 medals of assorted saints. Some were made from steel, some from oxidized silver, and others from aluminum. I came to visit one day, and Dad was sitting at his kitchen table with all his medals spread out in front of him. It looked like he was assembling a jigsaw puzzle.

"Why so many medals?" I asked.

"I don't know," he answered. "I like the way they look. They are cool. I'll enjoy them for a while and then sell some of the extras at the flea market."

After appreciating his medals for a considerable length of time, he took out a Ziploc bag from a kitchen drawer and put all the medals in the bag.

What I'm about to tell you sounds improbable at best—perhaps unbelievable. You might say it attests to the joy of collecting, or maybe it was a Christmas miracle. I don't know.

Three weeks before Christmas, my father's back went out. When he got out of bed that morning he could hardly move, and he couldn't stand erect. He was hunched over like Quasimodo. Each time he attempted to walk he was in agonizing pain.

Mother took him first to a chiropractor who only seemed to exacerbate the condition, so she brought him next to the family physician. Dr. Goldfeder pushed, pulled, and twisted him. All Dad could do was cry out in pain. Finally the doctor put my father on powerful pain medications. Then he wrote a prescription for my father to see a physical therapist. "If the therapy doesn't work after three sessions," the doctor advised, "we'll admit you to the hospital and run an MRI. It could mean surgery, but it's too premature to tell."

After a few days of bed rest, and while under the effects of the narcotics, Dad started his physical therapy regime. At first it was very difficult because he was so stiff. When the session ended Dad was exhausted. After he returned home he took more medicine and slept for three hours. The second session went a little easier and the third better yet. But despite the therapy, Dad still could not stand up straight and continued to use a walker.

On Christmas Eve, Dad was discouraged over his lack of improvement. "I may never walk upright again," he said sullenly. "What a terrible way to spend the holidays. I am an invalid." Then he asked me if I would get the Ziploc bag with the religious medals from his desk drawer. I asked why, and he replied, "I am going to put the bag under my pillow and pray that the saints intercede for me."

"You're kidding," I said. "You don't actually believe that stuff, do you?"

"I neither believe nor disbelieve. I'm playing the odds. I mean, it can't hurt, can it? What do I know about religion, anyway? Not much."

So here's where the story gets bizarre. The next morning when Dad awakes, he climbs out of bed and stands straight as an arrow. Doubting his senses he begins to walk around the house. After a few laps he announces to mother and me, "I'm healed. I can walk, and there isn't any pain! It's a Christmas miracle. Now I can enjoy the holidays."

"To what do you owe your recovery?" I asked.

"I don't know."

"Do you think it's because of those saints?"

"Not necessarily, but maybe."

"Is there any particular one to which you would attribute this victory?"

"No. I give gratitude to all of them. I think it was a team effort."

78

"Couldn't it be just a coincidence, or luck?"

"I suppose. Frankly, it doesn't matter. I'm better and that is the important thing. Therefore, I'm grateful."

"Maybe it was the act of praying itself," I suggested. "It must be cathartic to pray."

"Yes, I believe it is. Don't people say that God answers prayers? He certainly answered mine."

"That's what they say, but I'm not sure that I believe it. It could be the placebo effect."

"Yes...it could be, or maybe the placebo effect is God answering prayer. All I know is that something worked. For me, that's all that matters."

When the New Year arrived I asked Dad if he had made a new year's resolution.

"Yes," he said. "I resolved to stop collecting. Well, not stop all together, but to become more discriminating in my acquisitions. As I grow older I want to develop more of a philosophical mindset. It's not just stuff I'm after. If you accumulate too much crap, you become a hoarder. That's not good. Even I don't want that much stuff. No, I want to collect things that will help me develop my spirituality, my soul. I want to become more peaceful and centered."

"Is it working for you?" I inquired.

"I think so," Dad answered. He went to his desk and removed an object from the drawer where he kept his eBay treasures. "Look here," he said, placing the item in my hand.

"What is it?"

"It's a Tibetan Prayer Wheel."

"What do you do with it?"

"You spin it when you pray. It helps you focus so you can achieve enlightenment."

"I see." I wasn't sure how to respond. After a few moments I asked, "Anything else?"

"Yes." He reached in and removed a silver object about two inches long and handed it to me. It was embossed with Hebrew letters.

"What is it?"

"A Mezuzah."

"A what?"

"It's Jewish. You attach it to your doorframe. I think of it as a miniature work of art. It contains a piece of parchment which has words from the Torah written on it. That's part of the Bible."

"Yes, I know, Dad, but what are you going to do with it?"

"Put it on the doorframe, or course. It will bless the house and by attaching it I will be doing something righteous. I think."

"I thought you were a Secular Humanist? Isn't that what you always said? What about scientific inquiry, objectivity, and all that kind of stuff?"

"Nice words. They sound good. I believe a healthy skepticism is desirable, but you can't argue with results. You see how well I'm walking. I am no longer the crooked man I was a month ago. So I'm giving thanks. If I am skeptical of anything it's of Secular Humanism itself. I mean, what has it done for me? Nothing. It may be a politically correct thing to say, but they are just words."

"Well," I said. "At least you didn't have to travel to France and visit Lourdes to get your healing. You never left the house."

"I have a medal from Lourdes. Would you like to see it?"

"Not now, maybe later. You know Dad, it has occurred to me that maybe eBay is your path to enlightenment. As you said, you can't argue with results. Anyway, whatever, or whomever is responsible for your recovery, I am happy for you. You were a pitiful thing all bent over and hobbling around the house on that walker. You were old before your time. I don't know about prayer wheels or the silver thing you attach to your doorframe, but if they illuminate your path, then I believe they're a good thing. Think of them as spiritual aids. But I would reserve a little gratitude for the physical therapist, the person who pulled and twisted you. I'm sure that person played a part in your Christmas miracle."

Previously published in *The Whirlwind Review* (2013)

TRULY BLESSED
By Lynn C. Johnston

When I found more pain in others
Than I found within myself
I learned what it meant to feel compassion
And my pain began to fade

When I found more forgiveness in others
Than I found within myself
I learned what it meant to feel peace
And my heart began to mend

When I found more belief in others
Than I found within myself
I learned what it meant to have faith
And my fears began to die

And when I found more love in others
Than I found within myself
I learned what it meant to feel truly blessed
And my spirit began to soar

Previously published in *Angel's Dance: A Collection of Uplifting & Inspirational Poetry* (Whispering Angel Books)

GOD'S TOUCH
By Ronda Armstrong

I was a patient at St. Mary's Hospital in Rochester, Minnesota on January 13, 1999.

"That's it!" declared a member of the hospital intravenous team when another one of my veins collapsed. "No more tries." He sighed. I sighed.

"They'll start your IV when you get to surgery." He paused, looking at me with kind eyes. "Sorry about sticking you extra. Good luck with surgery!" The IV cart rattled out of the room with the two technicians close behind.

My dinky veins, which tend to hide or roll, have often presented problems when drawing blood or starting an IV. Difficulties with my veins during this particular hospitalization, unlike other medical adventures, led to clearer perspective about the care and compassion of medical staff.

The hospital chaplain strolled to my bedside. My husband Bill and I joined hands with him as he said a prayer for God to look over me and guide the surgeon's hands. After a last kiss from Bill, the transporter whisked me through the hallways to the preoperative area with the accompaniment of the cart side bars clanging and the whoosh of air hitting my face.

Waiting in a partitioned area with no pre-operative sedative was definitely a different experience. Wide awake as minutes ticked down, I wrestled with rising fear. Preparations to travel the 210 miles to Rochester and to be away from my job and our home occupied me in the preceding days. Receiving hugs and healing wishes from friends and family also kept concerns about the long, grueling surgery I faced at bay. Now I had nothing but time. And only my thoughts and observations of other patients and staff to fill my mind.

A portion of my stomach had been removed twenty-four years earlier due to rare tumors (today called GIST – gastrointestinal stromal tumors.) That day the surgeon planned to remove the remainder of it and form a pouch with a gastrointestinal loop. Adding to the complexity of the surgery, several liver tumors would be treated, as well as removing one adrenal gland full of a benign tumor.

Questions thrummed through me as I took deep breaths and attempted, not-so-successfully, to still my rambling mind.

I already habitually ate frequent small meals due to my first stomach surgery.

Would I still be able to eat anything I wanted without discomfort?

How long would it take me to recuperate?

Would I be away from my social work job for the whole semester?

Would the surgeon complete all he planned during surgery?

"Turn off the questions," I admonished. "Don't drive yourself into a tizzy."

A nurse in scrubs, probably close to my age of 47, stepped up to my bed. I'll call her Amelia. "Hi, dear," she said. "We just heard there will be a little delay before you go into surgery."

I shivered as I nodded, "Okay."

She retrieved a blanket from the warmer and tucked it close to my body while visiting with me about my home and family and job.

"Now let me know if you need anything at all. Waiting isn't easy," she added.

I watched her stop at another bed before my eyes darted around the room. I saw other staff as well as Amelia immersed in their duties, so lovingly attending to patients. Soft-spoken and soothing, they reassured and ministered to them. By the time more patients were rolled in, I believed the professionals resembled angels with an aura circling them. It didn't take much imagination for me to envision them as God's helpers on the edge of heaven. Gathering warm feelings in my heart and sending out positive thoughts for both staff and my fellow patients, replaced my runaway questions and fear.

By the time another delay ensued, the staff and I visited like old friends. "We like having an alert patient!" they said.

I responded with some of my best skills. I listened. I offered encouragement. I asked them to tell me more. I began seeing them as the unique and caring individuals who supported me during this tumultuous time.

Finally, the wait ended and my cart was rolled into the surgery room assigned to me. A nurse, probably a few years older than me – I'll call her Mary – met me with a light-filled smile. She touched her warm hand gently to mine.

"Ronda, I'll be with you through surgery no matter how long it takes." Then, as she started explaining the next steps, she lightly squeezed my hand, offering reassurance.

I smiled, whispering, "Thank you." She must embody the touch of God, I thought.

Dr. Thompson, my surgeon, and the rest of the team arrived. "Sorry for the delays, but now we're all set and we're gonna get you fixed up." We shared a few laughs as the IV needle slipped into my vein, this time without difficulty.

As the sedation started kicking in, I saw a note scribbled on the bulletin board above me. "Call Dr. Carney." A friend, and the pathologist who first named my unusual tumor disorder years before as Carney Triad, planned to observe the surgery. The fact that he would peer over me with his watchful eye comforted me. Floating into unconsciousness I felt confident I rested in God's palm, surrounded by a team of angels.

The next morning Dr. Thompson arrived in my room with a grin on his face and good news. "Mrs. Armstrong – You're gonna be here for the long haul!" I had no trouble believing his message transmitted the voice of God.

Fifteen years have passed since that miraculous experience and most of the years were healthy ones. The past couple of years my disease has ramped up and more treatments have ensued. Still dealing with disease or not, lack of sedation dulling my senses prior to surgery and slowing down the process on that bitterly cold and snowy day in 1999 taught me a crucial life lesson, one carrying me over many challenges since.

Every day, through ordinary and extraordinary circumstances, we creatures on earth create miracles by sharing God's warm heart and healing touch. I learned to discover God's fingerprints in every experience and to feel God's hand through everyone. God provides touches of healing and grace via all his helping angels. Now I know to notice and welcome these helping hands.

JOY AND SORROW
By Carole Abourjeili
Dedicated to Fr. Antoun Abourjeili.

Embrace your sorrows as you would your joy.
For, your sorrows are the seeds embedded
  in the garden of your happiness.
For, your greatest joys
  are *not* but the bloom of your sorrows past.

SALUTATION
By Judith Lyn Sutton

A field of gold
Brightens
In sunlight.
It is morning.
Dewdrops gleam
On a single thistle.
Salute the day.
Praise it.

MY DREAM CAME TRUE GOD'S WAY

By Sharon S. Fulham

"God speaks in the silence of the heart.
Listening is the beginning of prayer." ~ *Mother Teresa*

Sherri and I worked together as reading specialists for nearly 10 years in the elementary public school system. We were the best of friends. Many co-workers and friends were shocked and devastated by her diagnosis of Lou Gehrig's disease in June of 2012. Progression of this disease was rapid, yet Sherri always maintained a positive attitude, and lived each day to its fullest. Within six months, she entered the hospital with pneumonia, unable to speak or communicate, except for moving a few toes and fingers. Her daughter invited Sherri's friends to visit her in the hospital, and shared that soon she would be under hospice care.

The night before I was to visit her I was upset and restless. I wondered if she was ready for company, but her daughter said she wanted to see friends. I was in a quandary. In the early morning hours I had a vivid dream. Sherri appeared perfectly well! She walked toward me, energetic, and radiantly smiling. She wore blue and green spring attire and looked refreshed. Her hazel eyes twinkled with joy! She told me she felt so much better! Standing close to her seemed so real. I awoke light-hearted and eager to visit her! I hoped my dream was letting me know that she had vastly improved. I could hardly wait to see her radiant smile! En route to the hospital I purchased a beautiful bouquet of spring flowers, and drove as fast as traffic and road signs allowed to get there!

When I arrived at the hospital I discovered that she was worse. My heart sank... She was medicated and appeared to be in a deep sleep. Her husband said that every word spoken by us could be heard even though it appeared otherwise.

A calming peace settled over me as I went to her side. I gently squeezed her finger three times and whispered, "Sherri, I love you." She responded by squeezing my finger three times. I reminded her that she was not alone... that God was with her, and that her friends loved her and were praying. While holding her hand I softly prayed for God's comfort, peace and caring love, and that she would know He was with her. She began weeping softly. A few moments later her hazel eyes slowly fluttered open. A huge smile beamed across her face! I happily acknowledged her smile! Then ever so slowly her eyes closed as if she were resting... then once again opened wide with another amazing smile. I was aware that it took extreme effort for Sherri to open her eyes. I'll never forget those warm moving moments, and her beautiful smile which spoke volumes. My precious friend was letting me know that she had peace in her heart. God had indeed comforted her and calmed her fears.

Before I departed, I promised that I would return soon with friends that she wanted to see. Holding back tears was difficult for me as I walked out of her room. I wept en route to my car, broken hearted that ALS was slowly taking her. I was grateful that I had the privilege of letting her know I loved her.

Just six hours after I left Sherri's side, her husband called and tearfully related she had passed with a beautiful smile beaming across her face. Sobbing, my dream came to mind. It did come true, but it came true God's way! Sherri's pain and suffering had finally ended. She was now in heaven, radiantly smiling with boundless energy and rejoicing with loved ones.

Sometimes a dream can change the course of a day in an astonishing way. That's how it worked for me. I don't believe it was happenstance that I arrived at the hospital at just the right time to express my love to my dear friend, and to pray with her. I believe it was direct intervention from God through a dream which guided me. Sherri feared departing this life and leaving her family and friends. God soothed her heart and calmed her fears. I had no idea on that day, that it would be her home-going... but God did.

HE CARRIED ME
By Vanessa A. Jackson Austin

Though this year has been trying
And often time, I find myself crying,
He Carried Me.

As my body ached with pain
And my mind is stretched with strain,
He Carried Me.

Not knowing what to think
As my heart would sometimes sink,
He Carried Me.

While I was searching for an answer
God reminded me, *He is the Answer,*
He Carried Me.

Whenever I was let down
God would come around,
Because He can always be found,
He Carried Me.

For God carries me in His everlasting arms
As He reminds me, *"Do not be alarmed."*

Because He is with me every step of the way
And He delivers me with no delay.

So content I will be,
For I know God will forever…carry me.

Previously published in *Cries in the Wind* (WestBow Press)

WE ARE BLESSED

By William Lacewell, Jr.

You walk so your light will shine before men.
Your teachings strengthen us in spirit, to not sin.
You have been a role model we can look up to,
You walk in righteousness so we can follow you.

You preach to us on the way our lives should be,
Sometimes it seems the right way is hard to see.
I pray that you'll be blessed in all you do,
And that God will lead you, your whole life through.

You live your life as an example for others to see,
You set an excellent example, for someone like me.
Follow your true calling, in God's teaching from above,
And He will continue to bless you with His love.

I enjoy being in your presence and it strengthens me.
You've opened my eyes, to things I was unable to see.
You prayed for me and my troubles went away.
Now God has blessed us both, to see another day.

A SPIRITUAL AWAKENING:
THE FACE OF DEATH
By Judy Shepps Battle

I saw my mother two-and-a-half hours after she died. Her passing was not unexpected, but it was a shock. I came to the nursing home needing to be with her in this immediately post-mortem time – needing to be physically with her one last time; needing to absorb the reality that she was gone.

A somber nurse led me to the door of my mother's room and asked if I felt okay to see her alone. I nodded yes, although I didn't know what to expect, never having seen a dead body before. I took a deep breath and drew back the white curtains surrounding her bed. She lay there, blankets pulled up to her chin, seeming neither alive nor dead.

Her face had a faintly quizzical look and it struck me how pale, almost translucent, she looked. All wrinkles were gone, and she seemed smooth and ageless. Her jaw hung open, as if she were still able to breathe. Her nose looked too big for her face, and there was a bump on the bridge that I had never noticed.

"She must have broken her nose once," I thought, realizing that I couldn't remember the last time I had been so physically close to her that I could notice such a detail.

Her eyes were closed and very relaxed, but she looked as if she were watching something. Although the eyelids were shut, they had a focus -- unknown to anyone but her, yet definitely a focus.

Her forehead was mottled with three large patches of brown I hadn't ever noticed – like big liver spots. Her gray hair was wispy and brushed back. I realized there was so much I never felt free to notice about her. Fear had kept me at a distance.

I felt as I did nearly 23 years ago when the nurses brought Mike, my first born, to me. He was wrapped in swaddling clothes and I remember wondering whether it was all right to unwrap him. Now, I wondered if it was OK to touch my mother's body, remembering how touch had been absent from all our interaction when she was alive.

90

"You have a chance to do something different, Judy," a small voice whispered inside me.

I lifted the white blanket, took my mother's hand and held it. It felt heavy and rubber-like, but it wasn't stiff or even very cold. In fact, it felt the same as when I had held it on the previous Tuesday, except this time it didn't respond to my squeeze.

It was her face that drew me closer. I looked at it from many angles, trying to capture what her last thoughts and awareness might have been. I felt there was a message there for me somewhere – not a personal one from her, but a final lesson for me to learn.

I kept looking and looking at her. In death, she seemed no different from in life, other than there was no breathing. Well, sort of "no breathing." Several times I was positive her chest moved up and down; that the white blanket over her moved. I had the eerie feeling that she was going to start breathing again at any moment.

In death she radiated some of the child within her – a kind of innocence – and some of the young mother I remembered. She used to have a dreamy quality about her, able to build sand castles with me on the beach in Coney Island, and read bedtime stories with flair and drama. I wished I had known her better at that time, or that it had lasted longer.

I heard myself begin to say the Lord's Prayer, the standard closing prayer at my 12-Step meetings, and felt tears come to my eyes. As I said the Our Father, I felt Creator in the room. Each of the words had special meaning to this situation, to the torturous mother-daughter relationship we had in life.

"Our Father, who art in heaven, hallowed be Thy name. Thy Kingdom come. Thy will be done. On earth as it is in heaven ..."

"Yes, it has," I thought. "Yes, it has. My relationship with you has been guided by Creator's will. By both of us being obedient to the roles we had to play with each other in this incarnation. Maybe next time, Mom, maybe we can do it differently."

"Give us this day our daily bread. And forgive us our trespasses as we forgive those who trespass against us."

The profundity of those words leapt out at me. In death, the world of trespasses is passé. They are irrelevant. The lifelong game of accumulating injuries is over. The final score is tied between her and me. We each gave as good as we got. Neither of us was able to transcend the barrier. I tried in her last days, but her doors never opened, at least not perceptively.

I looked closely at the body in front of me and saw great strength and great beauty. As our war ended and our conflict-laden earth roles of mother and daughter faded, I saw the spirit of Gaia, earth mother goddess.

"And lead us not into temptation. But deliver us from evil. For Thine is the kingdom, the power and the glory, forever and ever. Amen."

I apologized for saying a non-Jewish prayer, and told her it had great meaning for me as part of my addiction recovery program. We never shared my 12-Step recovery. She wasn't someone who asked for help in any form.

I said the 23rd Psalm, and then sang a verse from the Catholic liturgical song "Be Not Afraid"*:

"If you pass through raging waters in the sea, you shall not drown,
If you walk amid the burning flames, you shall not be harmed,
If you stand before the pow'r of hell and death is at your side,
Know that I am with you through it all.
Be not afraid, I go before you always,
Come follow me, and I will give you rest."

I had sung that song to Tom and Katie, my two youngest children, before they went into the operating room to have their adenoids taken out and ear tubes put in. I heard a maternal croon in my own voice as I addressed whatever fears my mother's soul might have.

I was crying as I instinctively switched over to Hebrew, intoning the "Shemah Yisroal, Adonai Elochanu, Adonai Echot" -- Hear O Israel, the Lord our God, the Lord is one. It was an old prayer, left over from my elementary school days when we went to "religious instruction" every Wednesday afternoon. I felt a bond with Creator that transcended name, language, or religion. My cry to the universe was to wish Mother safe journey and God speed.

Finally, I said good-bye to her body and to her role in my life.

I left her body as I had found it, drawing the curtains as I departed. Later, the floor supervisor and I went back in the room to check for mementos. Her voice hushed as we drew back the curtains, and she tiptoed past Mother's body. I guessed I wasn't the only one who wasn't quite sure she was dead.

My mother's death-face is more imprinted on me than her life-face. In a curious way, it seems stronger and more human. I see more of her in me, and more of me in her. I used to joke that I must have been adopted because I am so unlike anyone in my family. Today I recognized my kinship with her.

She was always afraid she would die alone; that she would be a bag lady. The reality was that she was in a rather expensive nursing home, and there were folks with her who truly cared about her. I want to believe that in her last moments she conquered that fear and could feel safe. I want to believe that, at the end, she found and experienced cosmic love, and that was what accounted for the surprised look on her face in death.

I will never know the nature of her final awareness. All I know is that I am no longer afraid of death or dying. I was part of her last two-and-a-half weeks of life and each moment was gentle. Death waited until she was ready to go.

My dear friend Elizabeth tried to tell me about this facet of death; how, in her words, a "good death" was incredibly beautiful. I had thought her ghoulish, but I now know exactly what she meant. My mother had a "good death," and my life has been enhanced immeasurably by being present to it.

Namaste, my mother. The spirit within me bows to the spirit within you.

RECIPROCITY
By Paul Cummins
for L.R.

When she spoke,
gratitude washed over me, yet
sadness too, her comment
almost a benediction, but not
because of its soul-searing truth,
because almost immediately I
began transposing it into
my own personal keys,
all the while recalling
our four-decade connection.
She said, "I cannot imagine
this world without you in it."
Certainly the reciprocate is true.
There are, we all know, those few
in every life for whom
this is the measure —put simply,
they are not replaceable.

THE VISION

By Lorraine Quirke

A yell from my mother's bedroom frightened me. I raced in to see what was wrong. Mother sat in bed, upset and confused, trying to change the TV station with her remote. She struggled with the monster until her frustration erupted.

"I need help with this," she said. "I can't do anything anymore." I was in my fifties when my mother said to me, "Don't get old!" It tugged at my heart to watch my mom's mind and abilities slowly deteriorate.

Most mothers are wonderful, caring, and nurturing individuals—a beautiful gift from God. Mine was no exception. My blue-eyed angel from heaven showed me how to love, and by her example, showed me how much she loved the Lord. My invincible mom would live forever. But, as I grew into adulthood, I learned that wasn't true.

In a few short years our roles reversed. She could no longer take care of herself. She needed the care, understanding, and patience I had received all of my life. As she became frail, and unable to perform simple tasks, would I cave in when she desperately needed me the most?

Before long, my level of frustration started rising. She became childlike—mumbling and asking questions like a three-year-old. I repeated what to do constantly. She became forgetful, and forgetting disturbed her the most.

She also lost all desire to take care of herself. I had trouble getting her to eat and go to the bathroom. Sometimes, I would try to call her from work, but the phone was always busy. I would become worried and ask permission to go home, only to find she had put the receiver down backward.

I wanted to scream, but I handled it with all the finesse I could muster.

I tried to remain calm, but something would happen in my body; I would start shaking and want to run away. Had I short-circuited my

94

emotional wiring and warm feelings? I prayed to the heavenly electrician to straighten me out. "Fix the wires so I can feel compassion again."

After I spent time making a nice dinner for her, she complained, "I can't eat this." Other times she said, "Why don't you make ground meat? I can eat that."

I had to learn how to tune out many of her remarks, maintain a sense of humor, and be willing to sacrifice. I needed a sense of humor, when my mother thought I was her sister, and wondered why I didn't look ninety-three.

Because she never remembered to eat breakfast, I lifted my mother against her pillows and gave her breakfast in bed. My arms were the loving arms of our Lord wrapped around her.

Although I knew I was fulfilling an important role, every day risked becoming an emotional train wreck. I walked as often as I could. Exercise helped alleviate my constant nerves and helplessness. I became afraid to leave her alone. I didn't always know what to do for her. Tears flowed, and guilt attacked me, when I thought about a nursing home in the future. I had promised her, I would never send her away. But, how long could I keep that promise?

A bible verse popped into my mind that set me free of worry and fear. I repeated it over and over: "I can do all things through Christ who strengthens me" (Philippians 4:13).

My journey was sometimes agonizing and difficult, but many blessings filled my life along the way. Her doctor told me I was doing a good job. When my mother said, "I think God is pleased with you," it brought tears to my eyes, and confirmed I was doing the best for her.

She died at age ninety-two, and I am happy I made her last years bearable. Also, during this time, the Lord gave me a wonderful gift, the desire to be a writer.

During the funeral, I experienced God's grace and remained calm. But after several months, I began to feel guilty again. I remembered all the mean words I had said to her throughout my life. My tongue had caused pain; my words were sharp. It hurt to think that I had ever made her cry. My nerves jumped like Mexican jumping beans, and I was worried she didn't know I loved her. The thoughts pierced my heart. Guilt affected my working life and my personal life, too. I needed my friend, Jesus. I told him that if I could only see or hear from my mother, it would be great. The request seemed strange — and impossible. The Lord rarely gives us that kind of privilege.

One morning, before getting ready for work, I was about to get up when I saw a vision of my mother. She looked young and beautiful. For a minute I thought she was alive.

"Mom, is that you?" Was I in heaven? The vision lasted for a few seconds, and then disappeared.

She looked whole and happy. No more tears. The vision lifted my spirits, and the guilt I had wrestled with for months disappeared.

The Lord had given me a marvelous gift, and it confirmed what I had hoped. My mother did know I loved her. Even now, I am grateful it is the love that remains.

"Miracles come in moments. Be ready and willing." ~Wayne Dyer

OUR MIRACLE OF LOVE

By Sharon S. Fulham

I remember all those days and nights
How we yearned for a baby boy
 Even though we prayed and believed
It seemed an unreachable joy
I thought that time had passed me by
That perhaps it could never be
When it seemed all hope had gone
I joyously conceived
"Honey, we got us a boy!"
Your daddy voiced his song
Seven pounds three and a half ounces
You were twenty two inches long
When your hazel eyes gazed into mine
 I was dazzled by your charms
It seemed I could never let you go
 As I cradled you in my arms
I touched your tiny fingers and toes
While smiling through my tears
You inherited your mother's tiny lips
And your father's precious ears
You will always be our pride and joy
Oh, how we thank God above
 for giving us a son so dear
 Our miracle of love

FAITH

By Carole Abourjeili
Dedicated to Fr. Antoun Abourjeili.

Should one be blessed to see the light of day then,
 be sure to offer thanks at dawn and say:
"There is no God but the one.
Only God has created the heavens and the earth,
and all around them and in between.
For only God is commander of our fate in life.
For God is gentle, kind, and loving.
 For only God is able to forgive our abundant sins
    and accept our good by little.
For only God is able to bestow light from darkness.
Only God may bestow the light of days upon us,
just as the sun that touches the dark corners of the earth
to grant us its gentle solace and merciful grace.
For only God is patient, generous, and wise."

ABOUT THE CONTRIBUTORS

Carole Abourjeili – Carole is 32 and has a Bachelor of Arts. She started writing poetry in Arabic and French in Lebanon then a few years after migrating to Australia, at age 12, she began writing in English. Most of her poems deal with the supernatural theme and what lies beyond the unknown: "Each poem is a piece of my soul that I like to share with the world. For me, writing is a place where I find inner peace and connection with the Divine." Other Publications: *Fortune Teller, and Awakening – Spectual Realms,* Hippocampus Press, New York (2014); *Chanteuse – InDaily,* Adelaide (2014); *Furaq- Spectral Realms,* Hippocampus Press, New York (2015).

Debbie Acklin – Debbie, an avid reader and traveler, lives in Alabama with her husband, two grown children and Duchess the cat. During the last few years, she has become a prolific writer for anthologies, most notably the popular *Chicken Soup for the Soup* series, for which she is a top contributor. She has been interviewed on radio and TV for her work, as well as appearing in numerous newspaper articles. Her latest project is a first attempt as a novelist. You may contact her at d_acklin@hotmail.com. She also invites you to join her on Facebook: www.facebook.com/debbieacklinauthor, and Twitter: @debbieacklin.

Ranita Adams - On July 12, 2013, Ranita was diagnosed with HER 2 positive invasive breast cancer. She had two tumors in her right breast and one in her lymph node. To date, she has gone through 18 weeks of chemo therapy, a mastectomy, 5 weeks of radiation and most recently a tissue transplant to reconstruct her right breast. Inspired by her positive attitude, her oncologist asked her to write a story about her journey. The doctor featured her story as the first "survivor" story for the Alamo City Cancer Council website hoping to inspire other cancer patients.

Terrie Alvarez – TK Alvarez lives in central Illinois with her husband of many, many years and enjoys music, gardening, and most of all, writing.

After experiencing and grieving the proverbial empty nest, she realized she finally had time to pursue some long-forgotten dreams. This is TK's first published work and she is deeply grateful to her writers' group, Writer's Oasis, for their encouragement and positive critiquing. A special mention of her mother, now deceased but with her always, must be made because for many years she encouraged TK to write, write, write. Terrie.alvarez@gmail.com.

Ronda Armstrong – Ronda and her husband live in Iowa. They enjoy ballroom dancing, relaxing with their cats, and helping others. Ronda reads, writes, and supports the literary community due to her belief in the healing power of stories to connect and inspire-both writer and reader. Her work appears in varied anthologies, including *Chicken Soup for the Soul, Tending Your Inner Garden, Seasons of Our Lives,* , e-books from *Women's Memoirs, Story Circle Network's True Words*, as well as Whispering Angel Books' *Nurturing Paws*. Ronda rotates with other writers at http://thebridgemeditations.wordpress.com. Contact her at ronda.armstrong@gmail.com.

Vanessa A. Jackson Austin – Vanessa is an artist, author, poet, writer and two-time cancer survivor. Her poems, *Never Give Up* and *Talk to God* were featured in the 2009 anthology of Whispering Angel Books, *Hope Whispers*. She has published two inspirational poetry books, *Live On* and *Refreshments for the Heart*. Her latest book, *Cries in the Wind*, is an inspirational book chronicling her cancer journey. Vanessa also has a line of handcrafted inspirational greeting cards. Owner of CABBIT Designs, she lives with her husband and three sons in Harvest, Alabama. Vanessa can be reached at www.cabbitdesigns.net.

Judy Shepps Battle – Judy has been writing essays and poems long before she became a psychotherapist and sociology professor at Rutgers University. Widely published both in the USA and abroad during the 60's and 70's, she deferred publishing to concentrate on career and family. Fortunately her muse was tenacious and she continued to write during the next three decades filling a file cabinet with scrawled and typewritten material that are now being organized into books and individual submissions. This essay represents her return to active participation in the writing community. She can't think of a better way to spend her retirement.

Janice Canerdy – Janice is a retired high-school English teacher from Potts Camp, Mississippi, who has been writing poetry since childhood. Her poems have appeared in various anthologies and journals/magazines, including *The Lyric, Bitterroot, The Road Not Taken,*

True Romance, The Mississippi Poetry Society Journal, Lucid Rhythms, Encore: The National Federation of State Poetry Societies Journal, Cyclamens and Swords, Parody (Onimpression), The Southern Poetry Association Journal(s), The Atomic Comic, and *The Artistic Muse.* She is inspired to write by life in general and by her grandchildren and church life in particular.

Elynne Chaplik-Aleskow – Elynne is a Pushcart Prize nominated author and award-winning educator and broadcaster. She is Founding General Manager of WYCC-TV/PBS and Distinguished Professor Emeritus of Wright College in Chicago. Her program *IN HER OWN VOICE* is renowned. Her stories and essays have been published in numerous anthologies and various magazines. Elynne Chaplik-Aleskow's performances of her stories have been broadcast on *The Bob Edwards Show* on NPR, *Rick Kogan's Sunday Papers* on WGN radio and YouTube. She has performed her stories in NYC, Chicago, Michigan and Canada. Her work has been part of a staged production in L.A. A film short adaptation of Elynne's story "The Hat" was featured at a Chicago Indie film festival. Visit http://LookAroundMe.blogspot.com

Kim Chatfield – Kim was born and raised in New Jersey now lives in Sebastian FL with her husband She enjoys her life in FL with family and friends. She has her B.A. in Dance and taught dance and exercise for many years. Now she enjoys being a student of dance and she works as an accountant in FL. Thumbs Up is her first true story and is thankful to share it with whomever is meant to read it. She welcomes any communication at kchatfield32958@yahoo.com or 772-532-8864. She is now writing spiritual articles that she will submit to Christian and spiritual magazines.

William Creed – William has written six books. *Comes The End, The Gathering; The Promise;* and *The New Dawn* are being released as a set by 23 West Publishers. His other books are titled: *Faith: God's Gift* and *Creeds.* In 1980, he was bitten by a mosquito and contracted Encephalitis. He lost ability to read or write or understand the English language. Doctors told him he would not recover, but he did. *Married To a Nurse,* is a tribute to his wife, Sharon, who literally saved his life. She is, his chief fan and critic in his writing career. Visit him at www.williamcreed.com.

Paul Cummins – Paul is the Executive Director of Coalition for Engaged Education and has been the primary founder of many innovative schools and programs that have made Engaged Education accessible to children and youth from diverse backgrounds, including foster children and incarcerated youth. At heart, Cummins is a poet and a writer whose publications include poems that have appeared in numerous journals. His full-length collections of poetry are *A Postcard from Bali,* and *Under Cover.* Paul and his wife Mary Ann live in Santa Monica and have four daughters, two granddaughters, and three grandsons.

Daawy – Daawy says she is fortunate to have such loving family who support her constantly in her writing journey. The tears that glimmered in her father's eyes when he read her stories, *About A Smile* in 'Littlest Blessings' and this story *Still With Me* meant so much more to her than obtaining her LLB (Hons) Law Degree from Nottingham Upon Trent University. She is currently working on a fiction novel, which she hopes will bridge between the Arabic and English worlds. It will be published by the end of this year. Please follow her at http://twitter.com/Daawy or visit http://daawy.blogspot.com

Liz Dolan – Liz's poetry manuscript, *A Secret of Long Life,* nominated for the Robert McGovern Prize, will soon be published by Cave Moon Press. Her first poetry collection, *They Abide,* was published by March Street. A six-time Pushcart nominee and winner of Best of the Web, she was a finalist for Best of the Net 2014.

Terri Elders – As frequent Whispering Angel contributor, Terri wishes her late husband, Ken Wilson, were here to share in her joy that yet another of her stories has been published. She lives near Colville WA. Contact her at telders@hotmail.com. She blogs at http://attouchoftarragon.blogspot.com/

Quilliam Horace Flint – He is a reflective hound dog, having seen enough of life's difficulties to have sobered his views of the world at large. Since his adoption Horace has been composing verse and has dedicated it to helping others who have yet to find their homes. ALL of his profits go to the shelter who took him in (Wetzel County Animal Shelter in New Martinsville, WV) and the rescues that helped him gain this good life. In addition, he regularly supports other rescues and good causes with donations of his books and other items for fundraising prizes.

Sharon S. Fulham – Sharon's inspiration for writing began in the eighth grade when she won a Halloween poetry contest. Her writing became her lifelong companion following her to universities where she earned a BA in Religion, and a MS in Education. As a reading specialist, in the public school system, struggling readers reached their highest potential through her reading strategies. She turned her lifelong love of words into a budding "Personalized Poetry" business, writing and publishing over

102

500 customized poems. Her inspirational poems graced local bookstores, and her writing has appeared in The Upper Room. Sharon's greatest joy is to uplift others, and to celebrate life with her husband and son in NC.

Louise Borad Gerber – Louise has written about her life with her "special" daughter, Naomi, both in a memoir and in poetry. Whereas the memoir is the story of their intertwined lives, the poetry synthesizes the emotional impact, the truths, her realizations, and her ultimate acceptance. Louise has had her poetry published in several anthologies. One of her poems won first place at the Santa Barbara Writer's Conference. Louise's many careers include: elementary school teacher, mother, special needs activist, artist, and business owner. She can be reached via email: LouiseSBG@gmail.com.

Juley Harvey – Juley says, "Why A Poet? Why A Duck? Why do I write poetry? It's the shortest and quickest way to get what's in here, out there. I do it because I cannot not write. It helps me figure things out, Lord save us, since I can't be Queen of the Universe or Princess Quite A Lot." A former journalist, her poetry has seen the light of day in more than 30 publications. Currently residing in the Rocky Mountains with her faithful dog, Moosie, and her faithful 93-year-old father, the soul of the ocean won't be stilled and California calls, as ever. From the mountains to the oceans....

Carolyn T. Johnson – Her life has provided her many twists and turns over the years, but she subscribes the advice of a popular Lee Ann Womack song and when she gets the chance to sit it out or dance, she dances. Carolyn T. Johnson, a former banker and now freelance writer from Houston, Texas, writes from the heart, the hurt, the heavenly and sometimes the hilarious. Her work can be found in *The Houston Chronicle* and *The Austin American-Statesman* newspapers, as well as several Whispering Angel Books anthologies, *Chicken Soup for the Soul, Publishing Syndicate*, and numerous other anthologies and e-zines.

Lynn C. Johnston is the author of *Angel's Dance: A Collection of Uplifting and Inspirational Poetry* and founder of Whispering Angel Books. She served as editor for *Hope Whispers, Living Lessons, Nurturing Paws, Littlest Blessings, and Stir-Fried Memories*. Her poems and essays have been published in several anthologies, including *Forever Friends, Timeless Mysteries, Antiquities, The World Awaits,* and *Turning Corners, Bridges.* Originally from New York, Lynn is a graduate of SUNY New Paltz. For more information, please visit www.whisperingangelbooks.com.

William Lacewell, Jr. – William resides in Wilmington, N.C. He enjoys writing poetry for competitions. "Throughout life we encounter experiences that help shape our lives and our future," he said.. "We meet people that have a devastating impact on our lives and our emotions, both positive and negative." His poetry reflects on his encounters with such people through their life events, along with his own reflections of past memories and life experiences. Some of his poems reflect on the death of people that are very close to me. He writes about family members, in order to keep their memories alive for future generations.

Deborah LeFalle – Deborah has always liked to write, but only recently has begun to submit her work for potential publication. Poetry, narrative essay, and creative non-fiction are the genres she is drawn to most, with inspiration for her stories coming from personal experiences. She is a dedicated supporter of the literary, visual, and performing arts; and she enjoys spending time outdoors communing with nature. Deborah is an emeritus faculty member of Mission College in Santa Clara, California. She holds a Ph.D. in Transformative Studies.

Linda Lohman – For Linda, Sacramento, CA is home where she has a BA in English from Sacramento State University. She has been published in 11 *Chicken Soup for the Soul* books, two *Not Your Mother's Book* on (Dogs and Parenting). Additional publications include *Reader's Digest, The Sacramento Bee, Bead and Button, The Sacramento News & Review, Miss Kitty's Journal,* and *Solidarity*. Retired, she enjoys Red Hat friends, writing, reading, and beading. Her family and her Yorkie, Lucy, are her primary writing inspirations, but newspaper ads are fodder for her humor writing. You may contact her at lindaalohman@yahoo.com.

Rosemary McKinley—Rosemary began writing to both entertain and inspire others. Her book, *101 Glimpses of the North Fork and Islands* was released by History Press. Her short stories, essays, and poems have been published online by the Visiting Nurse Association of Long Island and in *Lucidity, LI Sounds, Clarity, canvasli.co114 Peconic Bay Shopper, Fate Magazine, Examination Anthology, Wormwood Press, Newsday, and The Poet's Arts*. Two short stories are available on smashwords.com Her Y/A historical novella, *The Wampum Exchange*, is set in 1650 in Southold, the first English settlement in New York State. It is available on Amazon.com and BN.com in print and ebook. Visit her at http://dreamlady-rosemarvmckinlev.blogspot.com/

Beckie A. Miller – Beckie has published numerous articles and appeared in *Forever Young, Unsent Letter, Writing as a Way to Resolve and Renew and*

104

Dear Mom, I Always Wanted You to Know. She is wife, mother and grandmother. She began writing after the murder of her 18-year-old son as an attempt to vent the horrific emotional aftermath of his murder. She has been Chapter Leader of Parents of Murdered Children (POMC) in Phoenix for the past 20 years, and has served on many crime victims' boards and organizations. She has also won numerous awards for her service to crime victims.

Harry P. Noble, Jr. - A native Texan, Harry grew up in Sabine County and graduated from San Augustine High. After two years in the military, eighteen months in Korea, he settled in Houston to begin his career in computers. He earned a Bachelor's in Mathematics and an MBA in Finance. Retired in 1991, he returned to San Augustine to write biographical history for the *San Augustine Tribune*. Digging into the local history, he launched a second career that has produced over a thousand articles and the publication of four books: *Texas Trailblazers; As Noble as It Gets; Schools of San Augustine County: A History; Me and Burnice,* and *A Simpler Time.*

Jim Pahz – Jim is professor emeritus at Central Michigan University. He writes alone, and sometimes with his wife, Cheryl. Their publications include: *Almost Chosen... Nearly Saved, Finding Quetzal, The Last Adventure Box, Lilith,* and *Saving Turtles.* All of his writings are available at Amazon.com. The personal website for Jim and Cheryl is jcpahz.com. He lives in Central Michigan with his wife, Cheryl.

Teresa Peipins – Teresa's poetry, fiction, and essays have appeared in publications both in the United States and abroad including *Anak Sastra, Barcelona Ink, The Barcelona Review, The Buffalo News, Conte, Creeping Bent, HawaiPacific Review, Melusine,* and *Pedestal,* among many others. *A Remedy of Touch* and *Box of Surprises* were published by Finishing Line Press and are available on Amazon. Her third chapbook of poetry, *Dance the Truth* was published by Saddle Road Press. Her novel, *"The Shadow of Silver Birch* is available on Amazon. She blogs at http://peipins.blogspot.com

Lynn Pinkerton - Lynn is a freelance writer who knew in the fifth grade she wanted to be a writer when she grew up. Sidetracked by careers in social services and special events marketing, Lynn eventually reclaimed her childhood aspiration, joined a writing group and began publishing. Her work has appeared in a variety of print and on-line publications including *The Christian Science Monitor, New Southerner* and *The Shine Journal,* as well as several anthologies including *Nurturing Paws, The Path* and *Littlest Blessings*. She divides her time between New Chapel Hill and Houston, Texas.

Lorraine Quirke – Lorraine is a retiree and writer with a desire to bring Christians into a deeper faith. She is a member of ACFW and Faithwriters. She writes talking animal stories for children, articles, and Christian fiction, including *Maxi Lights the Way*, published in October, 2010 anthology with Writers Group of the Triad. *Never Give Up* was published in the anthology *Living Lessons* from Whispering Angel Books. *The House that Seemed Alive* appeared in the October 2011 E-zine *A Flame in the Dark*. She resides in Chicago. She has two blogs: http://lquirke.blogspot.com, http://waitingfortheglory.blogspot.com

Judith Lyn Sutton – Judith, an award-winning poet, has had her poems appear in small press journals and anthologies nationwide with poems of luminaries such as Jack Kerouac, Adrienne Rich, Diane di Prima, Jane Hirschfield, and William Everson. Her work both as a writer and a teacher of poetry has received recognition at the local, state, and national level. She also has edited several books, including *Demons and Martyrs: Poems About Mutanabbi Street*, published in 2008 by Studio 1801 in Los Altos, CA. She draws inspiration for her poetry from nature and art which often speak to her of the whispering of angels.

Paula Timpson – Paula writes everyday Poetry for God's glory. Her 7-yr-old son is her Forever Muse. Paula has a Spirit Series of Poetry books as well as others listed on Amazon. Paula has her M.A. in Special Education and she loves helping others reach their potential through inspiration peace and love http://paulaspoetryworld.blogspot.com

Louise Webster – Louise graduated Magna Cum Laude with a degree in Communication Arts. Immediately after college she wrote the evening news for a small cable T.V. company. Staying home to raise her children afforded her the opportunity to write poetry for many of the small presses. She has also written an article for a psychology book, a horticulture magazine and won a contest on the history of Lake Ronkonkoma. Louise had poetry accepted by June Cotner for two of her anthologies *Dog Blessings* and *House Blessings*. She had a short story published in *Nurturing Paws* edited by Lynn C. Johnston. Most recently she has been a frequent contributor in *Tales of the Talisman* published by David Summers.

Cherise Wyneken – A freelance writer and Poetry Pushcart nominee, Cherise studied poetry and creative writing at FIU & FAU in South

Florida. Her articles, stories, and poems have appeared in a variety of anthologies, periodicals, and journals. She has authored poetry chapbooks, a spiritual memoir, a novel, a children's book, a children's audiocassette, and *Stir-Fried Memories*, published by Whispering Angel Books. After returning to the San Francisco Bay Area, she became involved with the Bay Area Poets Coalition, Women's Poetry and Potluck Salon. Cherise wrote a poetry column for the Oakland Examiner's online issue at: www.examiner.com/poetry-in-oakland/cherise-wyneken. To read more of her work, please visit http://www.authorsden.com/cherisewyneken.

WE WANT TO HEAR FROM YOU

Has one or more of the stories touched your heart? Has it made you think differently about your own situation? We would like to hear your thoughts or comments.

Do you have a short story or poem that you'd like to see in a future Whispering Angel Book? If so, please go to our website for upcoming book topics and submission guidelines.

Whispering Angel Books is dedicated to publishing uplifting and inspirational stories and poetry for its readers while donating a portion of its book sales to charities promoting physical, emotiona,l and spiritual healing. We also offer fundraising programs to help you increase revenue for your charitable organization. If you'd like more information, please contact us.

To contact us or to order additional books, please visit:

www.whisperingangelbooks.com

CPSIA information can be obtained at www.ICGtesting.com
Printed in the USA
LVOW11s0832290914

406339LV00001B/26/P